HIGH PLAINS PRESS

SINNERS
& SAINTS

Cover photo:
Patrick Doran (at left), his partner Svensen
and Doran's Irish setter
(Laramie Plains Museum)

SINNERS & SAINTS

∽ ∽ ∽ ∽ ∽ ∽ ∽ ∽ ∽ ∽ ∽ ∽ ∽ ∽

TALES OF
OLD LARAMIE CITY

∽ ∽ ∽ ∽ ∽ ∽ ∽ ∽ ∽ ∽ ∽ ∽ ∽ ∽

GLADYS B. BEERY

∽

HIGH PLAINS PRESS

Some of the chapters have appeared
in an earlier form in
True West magazine and
in the *Laramie Boomerang*.

Library of Congress Cataloging-in-Publication Data

Beery, Gladys B.
Sinners & saints: Tales of old Laramie City
Gladys B. Beery.
p. cm.
Includes bibliographical references and index.
ISBN 0-931271-24-X (hardcover: acid free paper)
ISBN 0-932171-23-1 (trade paper: acid free paper)
1. Laramie (Wyo.)—History
I. Title.
II. Title: Sinners and saints.
F769.L2B44   1994   93-38315
974.7'43—dc20   CIP

HIGH PLAINS PRESS
539 CASSA ROAD
GLENDO, WYOMING 82213

*This collection of tales
is dedicated to the real westerners:
the "little people" who lived peaceably and
toiled diligently and honorably
to make their homes in this wild, beautiful land.*

*They furnished the backs and shoulders
for the few to climb on in their quest
for riches and power.*

*We are the fortunate inheritors of their legacy.
May we be worthy to walk in their shoes.*

CONTENTS

⧜

FOREWORD

I N *SINNERS & SAINTS* Gladys Beck Beery examines the
antics and enterprises of early-comers to End-of-Track
Laramie City on the High Plains. "Probably the first
reaction of all newcomers to these great grasslands, stretching from horizon to horizon in awesome but frightening
beauty, was dismay," Beery says in assessing what was
given up and what was anticipated by those who laid out the
town. Some California/Oregon and Overland trail migrants
took root here, and others dismounted from the newly completed Union Pacific Railroad. Work was plentiful at the
new town site. "It was a bustling, noisy community," Beery
tells us.

There is no straight-line coherence in the way history
unfolds itself. The patch-quilt accounts comprising *Sinners &
Saints* effectively catch up Laramie's past. Beery's natural
storytelling skills in her pioneer adventure novel *Mule Woman*
(1992) and her historic insights in *Front Streets of Laramie
City* (1990) are joined in *Sinners & Saints*. It is a collection of
thirty-three sketches of the multi-ethnic characters shaping
Laramie from its post-Civil War beginnings to pre-World War
II. Each sketch concludes with a brief "Bibliographical
Essay," a descriptive account of the author's sources. An
array of period photos and contemporary note "Items" give
focus and pungency to the whole text.

The account begins with roistering shenanigans in the Shamrock Saloon, the Crystal Wine Parlors, the Bucket of Blood, and Chrisman's House of soiled doves. Tattered Indians and mountain men still stray among the frontier peoples in Beery's imaginative restaging of past events. "It is possible for tellers of tales to forget dates or mix them up," she admits, as she revisits Laramie's rough and tumble beginnings.

Then by degree she moves us toward stability and propriety in a history which includes the grogshop-courtroom impaneling of the world's first jury to seat women. These were a neglected population of homemakers, sharing the same streets with saloon keepers, merchants, and prostitutes. "Few ways were open to a woman of that era to make a living— either she had to become a cook or washerwoman or doxy," Beery laments.

"I have taken verbatim news reports to create the story and have also taken license in some instances suggesting a reason for certain actions," Beery describes her methods and motivations. The effect is a compelling blend of her own thoughts and the recorded words of the characters she presents: Patrick Doran, the Irishman who gave soldiers and civilians a place to drink and fight; Old Sherrod, a garrulous Nebraskan; Sitting in the Meek, a lost Indian; Milkman Mary, a tenacious German; Aunt Fronie, a skilled equestrian from Maine; Lady Bailiff, an English woman "of large proportions and commanding presence" in her court duties; John H. Hayford, dyspeptic editor of the *Daily Sentinel*; J.A. Edmondson, "the fightin' preacher;" Mrs. Jackson K. Brown, a headstrong Irish beauty; Bronco Sam, a black wrangler reenacting Othello's jealous murder of a pretty wife; Nettie Stewart, a winsome whore, and Susie Parker, a savvy madam; Katie, a girl bought "for a sack of flour;" the imperious Ivinsons; the moonshining Powells; A Man Named Roper, spouting Shakespeare to his cronies; The

Lone Bandit, gentleman Bill Carlyle. "A certain dark glamour surrounds an outlaw," Beery remarks elsewhere. And in that time's mixture of mayhem and morality, "Murder, while frowned upon," Beery wryly observes, "was not considered as serious a crime as horse stealing," distinguishing crimes of passion from cussedness.

"Many people scoff at the idea of ghosts," Beery says, but out of her own fervent belief in ghosts as messengers and precursors she shows us the Mist Walkers: "These unquiet spirits, whose highways are usually the night, thrive in Laramie. Sometimes there is only a subtle presence, but often it is a stronger manifestation. Some of Laramie's past residents have been seen in daylight in different parts of town...Men lost in the explosion of the railroad shops visit their old homes on the west side. Workmen and their ladies have been heard in happy talk in a house at the corner of Cedar and Sheridan... Spirits apparently select when and with whom they want to live, and when to leave," Beery surmises. We are glad for all the bodies and spirits she introduces in *Sinners & Saints,* and conclude that her particularized history of Laramie strongly resembles the generalized history of the settlement of the American West.

WALTER EDENS, PROFESSOR EMERITUS
DEPARTMENT OF ENGLISH
UNIVERSITY OF WYOMING, LARAMIE

SINNERS
& SAINTS

∞ *The end of the road for Asa Moyer, Con Wager, and Big Ed Wilson came at Laramie City, Wyoming, at the hands of a vigilante group of citizens.* (Wyoming State Museum)

𝕱 END OF THE TRACK

THEY DESERVED IT. Ever since the Union Pacific rails had reached Old Fort Kearney and Dobietown in Nebraska, the "sharpers" had run unchecked. At each end-of-track town their numbers grew. So did their lawlessness. Finally in Laramie City, Wyoming, some of the rowdies got what they deserved.

They had moved westward with the track. North Platte, Nebraska, was bad. Further west at Julesburg Crossing, the roughs ruled the town. When the rails were laid up along the Lodgepole Creek Valley many of the leeches followed. Others remained in Julesburg, running their games, plundering, robbing and murdering.

Julesburg was a crossroad. From there stages ran southwest to Denver City and the Colorado mines. Other travelers took the divide northwest over Jules Stretch to Fort Laramie and the Oregon Road. Emigrants still traveled the regular route to the west—up the Lodgepole Creek Valley, over the Black Hills [now called the Laramie Range], through Cheyenne Pass and out across the wide Laramie Plains.

With their successes, the rowdies became bolder and more careless. The final straw in Julesburg was their refusal to pay rent to the railroad on the lots they occupied. General Grenville Dodge sent an angry wire to Jack Casement, the U.P.

track-laying boss and a former brigadier general. The wire instructed Casement to take all the men he needed and go back and clean out Julesburg.

A fight was food and drink to Casement's Irish Gandy-dancers. Two hundred track-layers hopped onto the rail cars with Boss Casement and rattled down the Lodgepole Valley to Julesburg, all eager to tangle with the wily buckeens.

"The town is much quieter now," Casement later reported to his superior.

The track-layers rode their train back west nursing their bruises and telling and re-telling of the glorious time they'd had. The "element" remaining in Julesburg paid their rent.

At Cheyenne, the roughnecks followed the same pattern. Those who fled Julesburg joined again with their fellow hoodlums and others who had moved in. Robberies, garrotings, and the general fleecing of the public roused Cheyenne's law-abiding citizens. Jails weren't the answer. This required stronger measures.

The hanging of one of the trouble-makers, plus the posting of a sign warning "all evil-doers" of swift justice, spurred an exodus from Cheyenne—west again, with the rails.

The tracks were stalled for the winter of 1867 at Evans' Pass, more than eight thousand feet in altitude, atop the Black Hills. General Dodge re-named that point "Sherman" and the name Evans' Pass disappeared.

Sherman was a wide-open, roistering town all winter long. Tie cutters and other timber workers joined the railroad men and more money flowed.

Gambling, boozing and other types of entertainment were the rule of the hour. Women added to the offerings, and the men eagerly accepted.

Some of the sharpers moved on the few miles to Dale or beyond that to the town of Tie Siding. Tie Siding was where cross ties were stacked awaiting track-laying down the west slope of the mountains.

Since the track was laid at the rate of ten to fifteen miles a day, Tie Siding was not a long-lasting attraction. While it did last, though, it was like a huge burning torch, flaming hot.

Out on the broad Laramie Plains, Fort Sanders and the newly-platted village of Laramie City beckoned. And early in May 1868, the first train arrived.

In the mountains surrounding that valley were more than sixty tie camps. Each camp was composed of upwards of two hundred workmen. Their work created quite a thirst. And a need for relaxation. Also they found they frequently were attacked with bouts of *rheumaticks* which could only be cured with a good dollop of liquor. Maybe it was payday. Maybe a new idea on how to beat the tiger was burning in their minds along with the wages burning their pockets. All cures could be found in Laramie City.

In addition to the tie hacks and railroad workers, soldiers were stationed at Fort Sanders, located a convenient two miles south of Laramie City.

When these men gathered in town it created a glow, warmer and wilder than that at any of the other end-of-track towns.

The streets were laid out in Laramie City by survey but many of the first settlers pitched shacks or tents at random. A few put up sturdy, substantial buildings.

The first was the log building to house the *Frontier Index* and its newspaper equipment. There was space for the *Index*, living space for the Freeman brothers, rooms to let, plus a sample room.

A block west, facing the railyards, the entire street was lined with gaming and liquor rooms. The first to rise was Patrick Doran's Shamrock, a saloon-hotel. North of that was

Chrisman's House, boldly advertised as "Diana! Diana! The finest sporting house west of New York."

South of the Shamrock was the Bucket of Blood—a log building forty by forty feet with chinked walls, dirt floor and canvas roof. It was the headquarters for the leaders of the riffraff, Asa Moyer [also known as Ace Moore], Big Ed Wilson, Con Wager, Sam Dugan and a handful of the same type.

The carnival that was the new village flowed over fifteen blocks. The largest establishment, the Big Tent, stood on the corner at Second Street and what is now Ivinson Avenue. The Alhambra, transferred from Julesburg, was on Second, three blocks south.

Centre Street (following the English spelling) was not the center of town, but at the north verge. All of the action occurred south of Centre.

Payday wasn't a regular weekly event, but it was possible to "draw against your wages." A lot of relaxation could be found at ten cents a drink. A game of cards was free until you lost.

Nearly every dive offered music, dancing, and women. It was the duty of the women to dance with anyone. Dances were ten cents and short. The call "promenade to the bar" meant just that.

Day and night the revelry ran on, loud and rough. Daylight found bodies tucked away behind shacks, in boxcars, or in alleyways. Some breathed. Some had sore heads, bloody noses, missing teeth or oversized headaches. Others lay dead. All had empty pockets.

The Bucket of Blood was said to have bodies beneath its dirt floor and out in the backyard coal shed. Most tales related that numerous bodies were hauled out of town and brutally dumped into a ravine or washout.

Prudent men walked in the street with all senses alert even in daylight.

The first attempt at city government failed after three weeks. The roughnecks at once stepped into the breech; Moyer was mayor, Dugan the sheriff. The other gang leaders filled other city offices. Their control of the town was complete with Vice as their gospel.

By August, the conservative citizens were fed up. A group of twenty or thirty men met secretly in a back room of the Tivoli saloon and hatched a scheme to clean up the town.

This initial move ended with the hanging of a small-time goon called The Kid. The gang was now alerted and did some organizing on its own. They voiced threats of vengeance against any opposition.

Their grip on the town tightened. More murders, robberies, gypping and garroting followed. Bodies were found on railroad tracks, chopped up by the wheels.

Again the citizens met in secret. This time more than three hundred citizens came to the meeting. They planned carefully and organized meticulously. The date for action was set for the night of October 18, 1868.

Everything proceeded without a hitch. Squads gathered at assigned locations, and at a certain signal all were to attack.

Someone—relieving an itchy finger, or thirsting for glory, or to alert the goons—fired a shot before the appointed time and the whole thing erupted.

Screams, curses, yells and gunfire filled the night. One of the committee, one of the gang, and a musician were killed. A number of the desperados hopped onto a train, others left on horseback or with team and buggy. The direction didn't matter, just so it was out of town.

Three of the ringleaders were captured at the Bucket of Blood. Ace Moyer, Wager, and Wilson were marched across vacant lots to the unfinished cabin of John Keane at the corner of Third and what is now Kearney Avenue.

∞ The citizens of Laramie City seem surprisingly willing to be photographed with the body of Long Steve Young. The boy at the left is William O. Owen. (Laramie Plains Museum)

They were strung up on the projecting ridgepole of the cabin. The building was not high enough to make a drop. The trio were hauled up tight against the beam. Even so, their toes barely cleared the ground, so the drop did not break their necks. Rather, they strangled.

W.O. Owens, who was eight or ten years old at the time, had tagged along at the fringes of the action and related that the bodies bore several bullet holes in non-vital areas, so it may be the nooses were a more humane end.

Next morning another of the gang, "Long Steve" Young [sometimes identified as "Big Steve" Long] was caught and hanged from a telegraph pole near the railroad tracks.

The vigilantes then were disbanded, and Laramie City assumed a cloak of respectability.

∞

BIBLIOGRAPHICAL ESSAY.   J.H. Triggs, compiler of the first *History and Directory of Laramie City, 1875,* provided much of the information of the vigilante action in Laramie. His description is presented in the flowery words of the time. He mentions the "silvery dulcet tones of women's voices, fair though frail, yet woman still"; "the saturnalian festival"; and recalls the "sharp crack from deadly revolvers made music to the weeping and wailing of the women."

J.H. Hayford, editor of the *Sentinel, Laramie Daily Sentinel* and the *Weekly Sentinel* made occasional reference to the turbulent beginning of his Gem City.

Articles published as reminiscences of various early residents of Laramie City relate some of the happenings of the time. Each reflected the viewpoint and recollection of the person, thus giving sometimes conflicting accounts of the same event. An attempt has been made to combine the most relevant points to make a credible tale. This format was followed throughout this collection.

Reference is made to *A Work of Giants, the Building of the First Transcontinental Railroad* by Wesley D. Griswold (New York: McGraw-Hill, 1962) in the Julesburg action.

∽ ∽ ∽ ∽ ∽ ∽ ∽ ∽ ∽ ∽ ∽ ∽ ∽ ∽ ∽

FROM THE *CHIEF* IN HAY SPRINGS, NEBRASKA
REPRINTED IN THE *LARAMIE SENTINEL*

NOTICE!

THIS IS TO INFORM ALL CITIZENS OF HAY SPRINGS, AND ALL STRANGERS SOJOURNING THEREIN, THAT ON AND AFTER DECEMBER 1, 1880, IT WILL BE UNLAWFUL FOR ANYBODY TO CUSS, CAROUSE OR WHOOP.

THERE MUST BE NO MORE COMPELLING A MAN TO DRINK WHEN HE DOES NOT FEEL LIKE IT, NO MORE SHOOTING AT PLUG HATS AND NO MORE SHORT GAMES OF CHANCE. DRINKING FROM A BOTTLE MUST CEASE WHEN SALOONS ARE OPEN.

ANY MAN RIDING A HORSE INTO A SALOON WILL IMMEDIATELY BE SHOT. THE SAME WILL BEFALL THE MAN WHO COMPELS ANOTHER TO DANCE.

TIN HORN GAMBLERS AS WELL AS PROFESSIONALS ARE WARNED TO KEEP AWAY FROM THE TOWN. IT IS THE WISH OF THE NEW ADMINISTRATION TO MAKE THE TOWN LAW ABIDING. ALL GOOD CITIZENS ARE EXPECTED TO ARRAY THEMSELVES UPON THE SIDE OF LAW AND ORDER; ALL OTHERS WILL BE TURNED OVER TO THE CORONER.

∽ ∽ ∽ ∽ ∽ ∽ ∽ ∽ ∽ ∽ ∽ ∽ ∽ ∽ ∽

❦ Patrick Doran, Irishman

COUNTRYMEN HAVE a way of gathering. Tom Fagan, John Connor, M.H. Murphy, Patrick Doran and the three Fee brothers, all settled in the "Irish block" of Laramie City.

Patrick Doran built his hotel on Front Street in 1868, ahead of the railroad. He built of logs floated down the Big Laramie River from the forest above Sam Woods' Landing.

Young Doran, M.H. Murphy, John, Philip and Lawrence Fee and John W. Connor, all in their frisky twenties, came up the Platte River Road together in 1867. Fresh from Ireland by way of Canada, northern Dakota Territory and down the Missouri, the coltish men brought their small wagon-loads of possibles to pursue their rainbows in these broad new lands.

They went to work in the lumber camps of the Dawson brothers and learned the importance of mountains and the charm of their solitudes.

Spring brought Murphy and Doran back to Fort Sanders. Murphy went to work as chain-man with the surveyors of the new town site on the Big Laramie River. Doran built the log hotel which lost him a fortune.

Like a true Irishman, Doran named his hotel the Shamrock. In December 1869, it burned to the ground. Optimist Doran rebuilt, making it a bigger, two-story affair.

19

∽ *Patrick Doran owned the Shamrock Hotel which acquired quite a rough reputation in Laramie.* (Beery Collection)

It became the gathering place for the Irish and Swedish lads, in town from working in railroad or tie camps up in the forests that dressed the Rocky Mountains.

One of the legends about Patrick Doran concerns his method of keeping books. He had a slate-board hung on the back wall on which he wrote the customer's name and amount he owed. Any man arguing about his bill saw Pat wipe away the offense. Needless to say "wiping the slate clean" was a game played too often.

Patrick accepted all sorts of hard-luck stories. He was always ready to help a down-and-outer with a meal or a bed. No one ever went without if Patrick Doran heard about it.

"'Tis little enough to do, to help a man in need" was his philosophy.

And as to giving a man a bed, Patrick said: "Wyoming's weather is never settled. If it acts like it might, then sure and it changes at once. And everybody knows that our winter nights do get peevish."

Patrick may have been content—as years passed it would seem so—or maybe he shared the opinion of a countryman: "Now what would I want with profits? I have enough to live on."

His place soon acquired a reputation. On the rowdy front streets of the wide open town of Laramie City that was not easily done. But that was not Patrick's doing, for he was a mild man, not easily provoked.

One incident in the Shamrock Hotel had repercussions around the world. The story as related by various publications over the years seems to be wrong, according to court testimony.

The testimony states a quarrel broke out over a game of cards. Hot words led to gun-play. Although guns were ordinarily left with the bar-keeper, several weapons were apparently available. A man named Hoctor and Andrew Howie each had one. Possibly others were armed.

Howie and a man named Sutherland stood near the heating stove. Hoctor aimed his gun at them. Howie thought Hoctor would shoot and drew his gun.

Hoctor howled, "I'm going to shoot you!"

Both men fired and someone shot out the lamps in the barroom. When they were re-lit Hoctor lay dead and Patrick Doran was picking himself up from the floor, bleeding freely.

Tom Dayton, then boss at the railroad company's oil-house, went to his friend.

"Pat," he said. "I guess you're shot."

"No," Patrick replied. "I guess not."

The wound wasn't serious. With a good bandage over the affliction and a good shot of whiskey under his belt, Pat was well on the road to recovery.

The killing, however, wasn't so soon dismissed. It was the most prominent case put before that famous jury of 1870— the jury on which six women of Laramie City served. *(See later chapters in this book.)*

With the Irish, fighting was a pleasure taken as part of their nourishment. Add their usual evening pint, and sometimes their game became serious. And this brought on the "hard-name" given to the Shamrock and its owner.

Now Patrick himself was a mild man. See how he wiped the slate clean rather than argue. See how he was ready with meal or bed rather than question the supplicant. But there are limits, and Pat reached one in November 1872.

Editor Hayford reported it in his *Laramie Sentinel* "Sam Stone and Pat Doran had a row. Pat knocked Sam down and broke his collarbone. We don't know the merits of the case, but Pat and his house have a hard name, and it is safe to charge it to him."

Hayford continued: "If somebody would kill Pat they would do God-service, and we would give him an obituary notice that would surprise the natives."

Sam Stone was a brickmaker and no doubt had a pair of hard, rough hands. But Patrick laid him out and with a broken collar bone. It must have been a glorious row!

The hard name didn't detract from the Irishman's general reputation for honesty and common sense. His name appears often on jury panels. However, it also appears in city records on charges of drunkenness.

Like all Front Street saloon-hotels, the Shamrock had its girls. More than one "frail sister" departed this life either by accident or, more often, by design.

Sallie Thixton, a flaxen-haired siren at the Shamrock, was found dead in her unheated room at the hotel. A coroner's jury found the death "due to intemperance and exposure." Sallie had come to Laramie in 1868. According to the paper "...[there was] no one to hear her last words but a colored creature sunk almost as low as herself."

But that was *after* Patrick Doran had lost his hotel.

The slate had been wiped clean too often, there were too many free meals and beds. Pat was forced to borrow money to stay in business. He put up the Shamrock with its stable and other back-lot buildings, the two Front Street lots where they stood, and his homestead with its buildings as collateral. He could neither pay the taxes nor mortgages and in 1874 the whole was put up at a sheriff's sale.

His friend John W. Connor, proprietor of the Wyoming Hall on Second Street, and later founder of the Connor Hotel, paid off the mortgages and back taxes. He allowed his friend to continue living on the homestead and to operate the bar in his old Shamrock. There was no slate hanging on the back wall.

Hannah Murphy, sister of M.H., ran the hotel and dining room. In J.H. Triggs' City Directory of 1875, two advertisements appear for the Shamrock as "The Western House," giving both Hannah and Doran as proprietors.

Pat's hotel/tavern was a place where ranchers left word for hay hands or round-up help. He posted the notices and told the lads. And he looked at the lay-abouts, many of whom had cost him his property.

"Boys," he'd say. "There's hay to be got in. 'Tis a shame to waste a job."

Some would respond.

Hard as Hayford's words were against Doran, and much as he may have thought that Pat's demise would benefit the town, most Laramie people felt kindly toward the tall Irishman.

∞ An older Patrick Doran (left) is shown with his sometimes partner Svensen and his Irish setter. (Laramie Plains Museum)

When J.J. Fein shot Doran's horse, he was made to pay one hundred dollars for the animal, "though it was spavined." The homesteads of Fein and Doran bordered, and in the absence of fencing, livestock wandered where they willed.

Fein was another man in town who could do no good in the sight of Editor Hayford, so when a second horse belonging to Doran was shot and badly wounded, Fein was suspect.

Hayford printed: "It is getting about time some stop was put to the devilment going on here, or the press will begin to advocate, and the people to practice, Lynch law."

That wasn't the first—or the last—time the editor advocated lynching.

Patrick continued living on his farm east of town, raising vegetables and giving most of them away. Many went to Editor Hayford of the *Sentinel*, who dutifully expressed thanks in the newspaper columns.

Things were going poorly for Pat. In May, 1885, the *Daily Boomerang* reported the sheriff's sale of the contents of the old Shamrock barn. It "was attended by about half of the town. Every horse, wagon and set of harness was sold before noon. The stallion 'Centennial Gold Days' was sold to Peter Johnson of Red Buttes for $500. The silver-tongued auctioneer of the Rockies, W.W. Russell, conducted the sale." This, of course, was before Russell's silver tongue was quieted behind bars for selling stolen horses.

In 1912, W.S. McIntyre wrote of his respect and affection for his friend Doran "that gentle, unassuming man, clothed in a faded, black overcoat belted with narrow leather strap [who] greets all he meets in a strangely high-pitched voice" in which still lingered a touch of Irish brogue.

By that time fortune had dealt most harshly with the tall thin man who followed his pipe around. Due to friend Connor's promise, Doran continued to live on ground he had once owned, but Connor had sold the Doran homestead. It became the county fairgrounds and Patrick dwelt in two dumpy, drafty rooms under the grandstand. The county fairgrounds occupied the site where Newman Center now stands.

Each morning the sixty-seven-year-old Patrick would crawl under the barbed wire fence and walk the long way to town. Sometimes it took him a while to creep under the fence and get to his feet, but he went daily for any mail he might have and to meet his friends downtown.

Even with his meager means Patrick usually had some hobo or down-and-outer as guest in his small quarters.

For Patrick Doran still "had enough to live on" and he felt rich. He had his cow, one or two horses and a herd of hogs running on the open land south of the fairgrounds. The hogs were fattened and ready for market when cholera hit and within a few hours the entire herd was wiped out. But Patrick didn't whine. He still had his milk cow and horses and his dogs—the beautiful red setter who had been his companion for years and six or so strays he had befriended.

"He would hitch one of those scrawny horses to his little cart and drive around town cleaning the used bedding out of the barns. He hauled that soiled straw to his place and put it out for his stock to eat. It's no wonder they were nothin' but skin and bone," Jacob Berner said in a 1978 interview.

He asked no one for help, nor, apparently, did anyone remember that Patrick had helped them over some rough spots.

Patrick Doran spent his last five years living at the County Poor Farm, site of present-day Bethesda Care Center. Years before, the land had been part of his homestead where he grew the "sweetest vegetables in town."

Pat's hotel outlived the kindly Irishman. In 1926 the old Shamrock was condemned as a fire hazard and torn down for use as firewood.

If someone had asked Patrick if he had ever reached his rainbow's end, he would have laughed and replied: "Shurre, and I have that." For his old homestead is now an important part of Laramie known as the Rainbow Addition.

∞

BIBLIOGRAPHICAL ESSAY. Information on this beloved Irishman is found in the *Daily Sentinel* and *Weekly Sentinel* and in the *Boomerang*.

A 1978 interview with Jacob Berner, shortly before his death, provided some information.

Letters and columns of reminiscence by W.E. Chaplin and J. Ingersoll gave other information and repeated that of early research.

An item appearing in "Our Yesterdays" column in Laramie's *Daily Boomerang,* February 1890, relates, "The ugly hole in the east wall of the city jail which the prisoners used for their escape Monday was filled with baled hay. It was thought the problem was solved but Pat Doran's horse came along and ate up the hay."

∞ ∞ ∞ ∞ ∞ ∞ ∞ ∞ ∞ ∞ ∞ ∞   ∞ ∞ ∞

FROM THE *LARAMIE SENTINEL*
NOVEMBER 1890

"IN THE CENTENNIAL VALLEY IN NOVEMBER 1890, A MAN WRAPPED HIS FEET IN GUNNY SACKS AND STARTED OUT INTO THE MOUNTAINS TO HUNT. TWO OTHER HUNTERS RAN ONTO THE STRANGE TRACKS AND STARTED IN PURSUIT OF THE WILD CREATURE, WHICH THEY ASSUMED WAS A BEAR OR A STRANGE MONSTROUS MAMMAL OF SOME SORT. AFTER A LONG TIME THEY CAME TO A PLACE WHERE THE CREATURE HAD STOPPED TO REST, LEAVING A COPY OF THE NEWSPAPER, THE *BOOMERANG,* AND OTHER EVIDENCE OF CIVILIZATION. TWO FELLOWS HAD BEEN COMPLETELY SOLD!"

∞ ∞ ∞ ∞ ∞ ∞ ∞ ∞ ∞ ∞ ∞ ∞   ∞ ∞ ∞

❧ OLD SHERROD

H E WAS CALLED *"Old* Sherrod" while still in his early thirties—a designation usually bestowed by comrades out of respect and affection.

James Sherrod claimed the name was tied to him in Plattsmouth, Nebraska, when he performed a daring rescue from the ice-filled Missouri River.

That trick river often froze over in winter to such a depth that teams and loaded wagons could cross over, thus saving the cost of the ice-ferry.

This adventure came about when a man with three yoke of cattle started to cross from the Iowa side. The ice broke and the whole outfit fell into the water. A crowd gathered, but strangely no one moved to help the man. Sherrod's outfit was nearby; he called for help to get his lead wagon and one yoke of cattle out of his string so he could try to save the man. He succeeded in getting the man and his outfit out of the water, but as they turned toward shore, the ice gave way again and they all went into the river. The swift current carried them downstream for over a half mile, then turned them shoreward. They finally were able to crawl out onto the bank.

"By that time, there were about a thousand people watching us, and when my feet struck ground again I waved my hand at them, and they cheered me wildly. There was nothing

James Sherrod, a Laramie character, once performed a daring rescue from the ice-filled Missouri River. (Wyoming State Museum)

too good for Old Sherrod (in that city) that day! I've been called Old Sherrod every since...."

Sherrod loved a good story and told his with as much flair and color as the veriest mountain man. One of his best concerned Chief Crazy Horse.

Sherrod admitted that Chief Crazy Horse was the only Indian he was afraid of. The two had long feuded, each trying to outmaneuver the other and "get" him.

Sherrod said he would only go for the Indian "in a fair fight." He said, "Crazy Horse kept out of my reach out of respect" for his shooting ability.

Sherrod told that along in 1875 he was at Fort Laramie on his way back from the Black Hills gold camps. An Indian by the name of Big Little Man, friendly to the officers at the fort, came in and told them that Crazy Horse was going on the warpath again.

Sherrod, who often served as a government guide and scout, was asked to take a company of soldiers to White Clay Island near Fort Robinson, to take Big Little Man along, and to bring Crazy Horse in.

Sherrod and the company reached White Clay Island and "had Crazy Horse surrounded before he even knew we were in the country. He made no fuss, but came with us willingly enough. Down the road, suddenly, with no real warning, that old rascal made a lunge at Big Little Man and almost severed one of his arms with a big knife he had concealed on his person that we had missed in our search of him. Two soldiers right behind Crazy Horse ran him through with their bayonets when he attacked Big Little Man. The old Chief died in about two hours, long before we reached Fort Laramie, but we took him in anyway."

Like Jesse James and other well known figures, Crazy Horse died more than once. A year later, the wily chief was alive and fighting at the battle of the Little Big Horn against Custer. In May 1877, after a long winter of hardship and suffering when their food, shelter and clothing were burned by the U.S. Army, the chief and his Oglalas came to Fort Robinson [the Red Cloud Agency in Nebraska] and surrendered. He did die that time, of stab wounds—either from a bayonet or from another Indian's knife.

Sherrod was not there. But that didn't spoil his story one whit.

Many of his adventure tales were of Indian fights and escapades. The battles were either short and sweet, for Sherrod's "shooting arm was respected by all," or fierce, with reds outnumbering the whites. Often he mentions that the dead

Indians and ponies were piled "as high as a wagon." As were the thrills of his many adventures.

Old Sherrod married a beautiful Cherokee woman in Oklahoma. Historian Coutant says the marriage took place "sometime in the forties" and that Sherrod was in the Rocky Mountains in 1848. Sherrod gave the year he first reached the west as 1852.

In 1868, Old Sherrod brought his family to Laramie City and settled on land upstream on the Little Laramie River.

He made two summer trips to the Black Hills, he said, and came away each fall with around eight hundred dollars in gold. The second fall, on his return, he was robbed by the Blackburn-Pelton gang, so that year was a total loss.

He decided to stay awhile on his ranch, located about twenty miles from Laramie City

"I took contracts for hauling ties [for the Union Pacific railroad] or freight or mining supplies—any kind of work that came my way. I had quite a few head of stock by that time, both cattle and horses, and also quite a family of children. My wife was a Cherokee—the handsomest woman in the Chero- kee Nation....

"I had put up a lot of hay...on my ranch, and while busy with the hay, my cattle had strayed away from the ranch. The morning after I'd finished with the hay, I saddled up and took out looking for my cattle. Along the middle of the afternoon when about twenty miles from home, I rode up onto a little knoll to take a look about the country and discovered great clouds of smoke rolling up in the direction of the ranch. I knew the Indians had got to my ranch, and fully expected them to butcher my whole family."

Most outdoorsmen tell time by the sun, but Sherrod, of course, was different: "I took out my watch to see if I could reach home before dark, found I had about two hours of good daylight, and I rode that twenty miles in one hour and thirty-five minutes. When I came within sight of the cabin and saw my wife and baby in the door I was overjoyed...all my hay and half my corrals were burned, but my family was safe. Two old prospectors had come to the house for protection, and I presume that was what saved my family."

Sherrod apparently spent little time at home. He did considerable prospecting, carried mail, and worked for the army carrying dispatches—and dodging Indians, as well as shooting them and piling them "as high as a wagon."

One adventure occurred along Horse Creek, east of Laramie City, with Billy Carmichael. Billy shot a deer and was shot at by an Indian, but after a long chase Sherrod caught the Indian and took his horse.

"A real dandy [the horse] was. I sold him in Omaha afterward for $205. The buyer turned right around and sold him for $325. He was a Kentucky bred horse, and that Indian had either butchered some poor emigrant and taken the horse or else had stolen him in some way...."

He told that tale again and sold the horse; this time for more.

Old Sherrod was in Laramie City the night of October 18, 1868, when the vigilantes went to work.

"That night the vigilantes captured and hung four of the worst toughs. They would have finished up more of them, but they had been warned and hid or got on out of town." He names Big Ed, Ace Moore, Jack Hayes and one known as Shorty, who he said was the worst of the bunch. Con Wager was actually the man who was hanged, not Hayes, but Hayes was involved in a shooting scrape at a different time.

In another story Old Sherrod related how some of the boys out in the forest got up a dance at a tie camp near Sherrod's ranch. They brought some women out from town, and the party was going very well when someone started a row.

"Guns began to pop all over the place. Fist fights were rare them days—it was either guns or knives," Sherrod recorded in his memoirs. "It was getting pretty lively around there when the notorious Jack Watkins took a hand. His gun misfired three times in succession, something it had never done before, Jack said, and the fellow he was shooting at, or someone else in the crowd, got Jack in the hip. He got outside somehow and made for my stable and hid in my haystack. When he didn't show up in the morning the boys were all afraid to check out the stack—for Jack was a dead shot, and everyone thought his gun might not misfire again.

"Finally I went out. He was just crawling out of the stack. I said, 'Hello, Jack, you're not dead yet, are you?' 'No,' he replied, 'but I'm pretty well used up.'

"I took him up to the house and dressed his wound and kept him there until he recovered, which didn't take long."

That summer, Watkins got into another scrape at the courthouse and wounded both the sheriff and under-sheriff trying to help out a friend named Rogers. The pair escaped. A posse went chasing after them to no avail. Later on a message came from Rawlins. Watkins was there in jail. Did Laramie want to pay his fine and transportation back to Laramie for prosecution?

No, Laramie said. Keep him.

Sherrod heard no more about Watkins. He voiced his suspicion, however, that someone had tampered with the man's gun at that dance, hoping to get him killed.

Old Sherrod owned eighty acres on the south edge of town. He built a house there. Across the street west was another house which he owned and rented out to a saloon-keeper.

Will Owen, in a letter written in 1939 to a Laramie friend, related the following:

"The south limits of Laramie was an east and west line

south of the spring brook...which gave Laramie its water supply. Immediately south of this line...outside the city limits, stood a disreputable house where liquor was sold ad lib. It was a saloon of the type so common in those days, and stood just west of the county road running from Laramie to Fort Sanders...a tough joint...a notorious resort for the soldiers at Fort Sanders. It was known as Sunnyside. Shootings, knifings and other fights were a common thing there. Sherrod and his family lived across the street. His wife Nancy Jane, a Cherokee, was a real character. Civilization had not diminished her love for bright colors! I've seen her many times in the Sunnyside with her three or four daughters, all decked out in a rainbow of gaudy colors and ribbons. They didn't go there for a drink or to join in the antics, but for the company and laughs.

"Sherrod was a frequent visitor too, but rough and woolly as he was, he never touched liquor! He was strictly a law-abiding citizen, always obeyed all the laws. This may account for his unusually long life. He died in Carbon County at the age of 107!"

Owen also relates in his own memoirs Old Sherrod's brush with politics.

"[He] was a rugged frontier type, as tough physically as any one I've ever known. He was one of Laramie's most noted characters—not a product of schoolrooms, nor the sort of man you'd pick for mayor of this city.

"Jack Connor, a leading citizen, had already been nominated for the office by the Democrats. As a joke someone printed a lot of tickets with the name of James M. Sherrod for mayor. [Tickets could be made up by anyone for anyone at that time and distributed before the election—no fees nor financial backing necessary.]

"No one really took the Sherrod name seriously, but when the votes were counted Sherrod had drawn even with Connor, and stayed that way until the very end. The final tally showed Connor the winner by the slimmest of margins."

So by the thinnest skin, Old Sherrod escaped becoming a politician. Just goes to show that a really honest and trustworthy man didn't have to spend a fortune to be noticed.

∞

BIBLIOGRAPHICAL ESSAY. Some references to Sherrod are made in the *Laramie Sentinel*. More information was gleaned from the history of the Overland Trail compiled by Daniel Kinnaman of Rawlins, Wyoming, and the Whittenberg Collection at the American Heritage Center at the University of Wyoming. The memoirs of W.O. Owen provided additional information. Reference is made to Sherrod's own tale as it appears in an early *Annals of Wyoming*.

❦ SITTING IN THE MEEK

H E WAS A MAN OF different names. His birth name was Washinun or Black Spot. Black Coal Ashes, White Crow and Thunder were names given to him at various stages of his life. According to tribal custom, names were given in recognition of some daring or generous act. Another of his names was Vash. As he grew older he was called Sits In The Corner And Keeps His Mouth Shut. Because one who is quiet is thought to be meek, he was later given the token of deepest respect by his tribe with the beautiful name of Sitting in the Meek.

He was lost from his Arapaho family and found by Thomas Fitzpatrick and William Sublette as they traveled along the upper Cimmaron River Valley in southeastern Colorado. Fitzpatrick and Sublette were traveling with a caravan of trade-goods headed for Santa Fe markets.

The traders took the starving waif along to Santa Fe, nursing him back to health, teaching him their language and teaching him that not all white men were evil.

Fitzpatrick adopted the lad and named him William for Sublette, and Friday for the day he was found. Of all the names the lad held during his lifetime, he seemed to prefer Friday Fitzpatrick. Throughout the west he was famous merely as Friday or Chief Friday.

When the mountain men returned to St. Louis, Fitzpatrick found a home for the boy with friends there. Friday learned to read, write and cipher. There have been disputes as to how long he stayed in St. Louis and how much he learned. The most sensible and reliable reports say that he spent winters there and summers with the mountain men.

It is certain that Friday learned to love and trust his white friends. He learned to read and speak English fluently and became adept in many of the social graces of the period.

He also enjoyed smoking cigars.

On one of the summer trips, Friday's natural parents learned their son was alive and persuaded him to return to the tribe. At first he objected, saying his only family was the white people. He finally consented when he was convinced of the many ways in which he could bring about good relations between his two families.

Stories of Friday are numerous, yet he remains a shadowy, mysterious figure in western lore. His influence with his two families was successful in limited ways.

The Europeans brought with them their Old World premise that "What I can take is mine," with no thought given to those they trampled on. History would have a different flavor had the many treaties and promises made with the natives been kept .

Political powers changed frequently and promises made in good faith were often later ignored or scrapped entirely.

In some respects tribal philosophy was similar. The chief who signed anything spoke only for himself unless his immediate followers agreed to his actions. What one chief agreed to was not held binding on the chief or members of another group.

Friday understood both white man's thinking and the need for individual freedom of his native family. He directed his efforts toward promoting peace between his two families.

∞ Sitting in the Meek, as he was called in his later years, had many names throughout his life. (Beery Collection)

Friday was not a tribal chief. The title was bestowed upon him by white men with whom he was associated. His bravery, hunting skills, dignity and general deportment seemed to warrant this respect.

When Friday married, according to one source, he took four sisters as they reached marrying age. Since families tended to congregate, most of his little band were related. The numbers in his group varies, according to available sources. Editor Hayford of the *Laramie Sentinel* gives the usual number as "85 tepees camped on the Laramie Plains."

Friday's people greeted the first train to Laramie as it screamed its way down the long grade from the southeast out onto the grassy plain. The Indians sat on their horses or stood and stared in amazement at the mechanical monster pounding along its iron tracks, belching great streamers of black smoke into the tender blue sky.

The shrieking of the steam whistle was background to the shouting and shooting of the passengers seated on their wares and goods piled atop open rail cars. Other passengers, quieter and more dignified, sat in fairly comfortable surroundings inside the cars.

The Indians' ponies reacted wildly to this unusual racket, racing, pitching, snorting. Some were well controlled by their amazed riders who were certainly unaware of what this new intrusion meant to their beautiful, free homeland.

Friday and his Arapahoes spent summers on the plains of the Laramie basin and winters south in the valley of the Cache la Poudre. They lived on the rich river bottom known as Indian Meadows and spent time hunting in the mountains above the Poudre stream and squabbling off and on with the Utes who ranged on the west side of what is now Chambers Lake and the Rawah Mountains, in Colorado's beautiful North Park.

When the United States government set up the meeting at Fort Laramie which brought about the Treaty of 1851 and the thousands of Indians gathered, the white men, fewer than two hundred, were understandably nervous. The presence of the friendly Arapaho under the competent leadership of Friday, "a handsome young brave," helped to ease some of their fears. His skill as an interpreter, the respect in which he was held by the tribes, and the rapport between him and the mountain men were factors in the smoothness with which the meeting progressed.

The ten thousand Indians gathered on that site was a spectacle of grandeur and wild beauty. The knowledge that these tribes of so-called *savages* could come together and exercise the discipline necessary to keep peace, even when many ancient enemies sat in the same council circles, was a lesson no white man should have forgotten. Yet they did. Too many were unaware of, or cared nothing for, the sensibilities of the natives.

But the Indians were anxious for peace with their white brothers, even though many were distrustful. So the agreement was reached to grant passage to whites through their homelands. Even then, white settlers were moving in on the lands designated for the tribes, and the federal government made no effort to stop them.

After Colonel Chivington's men murdered the Cheyenne Indians camped with Black Kettle at Sand Creek in Colorado, Indians set about avenging the slaughter. Friday remained in the Poudre River area near present-day Latham-Greeley, and saw to it that his own grown sons did not join the avengers. Even Hayford later admitted that Friday's influence had averted more drastic retaliations.

On the recommendation of Colonel Albert Gallatin Boone, Colorado's Governor Evans refused to allow Friday and his tribe to continue living along the Cache la Poudre. Six white families had settled there, and the "lazy Indians would not plow nor grow crops on the fertile bottoms." Friday paid the Governor a visit and asked to be allowed to stay, but Evans refused the Arapaho's request for his "home grounds."

Even this refusal, which became final in 1869, did not turn Friday against the whites. But he was becoming bitter and frustrated. He did not harangue his braves so much for their actions against whites on the field of battle.

The tribes and white settlers did not even agree on what "war" was. Editor Hayford had gone with Friday on a horse raid against the Utes in upper Colorado and wrote a scathing account of the action. The Indians had not killed the Utes, he wrote, and sang only of their "victory" in stealing many horses.

Tribal warfare was deemed a contest of skill, not for murder. Its goal was to test the bravery of a warrior. The ability to touch an enemy without injuring him or being injured in return was one of the highest attributes of a warrior. "Counting coup" was an act few whites understood. This was what Hayford scorned. But the editor of the *Sentinel* had no sympathy for Indians.

After the refusal of Evans to grant Friday his homelands, Friday and his people joined the Northern Arapahoes under Medicine Man.

When the new Territory of Wyoming was created in 1869, Friday visited Governor Campbell and asked that he and his followers be allowed to settle on part of the Wind River Reservation with the Shoshones. Chief Washakie objected, saying that, although he and Friday were old and good friends, there were many bad Arapahoes and there would be trouble.

Friday visited Laramie and observed Hayford printing his newspaper the *Sentinel*. He did not remain long, for now the beautiful Laramie Plains were overrun with ranches, the Union Pacific Railroad and the evils that came with it. Nor did he return to his beloved Indian Meadows of Northern Colorado which was now "too good for the lazy Indians."

He traveled northward into upper Wyoming and Montana. Everywhere he ran into white men and their scornful and rude attitudes toward the Native Americans. Disheartened that his efforts at building peace and brotherhood between his two families had come to nothing, Friday again approached the Shoshones for permission to live on the reservation with them.

Washakie was now facing the reality that the Shoshone were "caged" on the reservation and that all tribes were destined for a similar fate. He consented to sharing the reservation with Friday and his people.

Even though disappointed, Friday still did not allow his immediate tribe to take part in any of the battles or raids against the whites. Although there were many temptations and many wrongs, Friday held steadfast in his loyalty to his white family. He served as interpreter whenever asked and acted in any other capacity within his powers.

Early in his life the Arapaho was noted for his intelligence, honesty and sobriety. Now, reports grew that Friday was reverting to the early primitive ways, the old teachings and taboos. Perhaps he felt that there was no future for his work and hopes. Also, his health was no longer robust. Rumors said that he was often drunk. Whiskey was claimed to be a pain-killer. It also numbed the mind against unwelcome memories.

William Friday Fitzpatrick died in May 1881, of kidney or heart disease, still grieving for his lost homeland and his failure to foster brotherhood between his two families.

Truly Friday had earned his evocative names—Sits in the Corner and Keeps his Mouth Shut and Sitting in the Meek.

∞

BIBLIOGRAPHICAL ESSAY. J.H. Hayford, Editor of Laramie's *Daily* and *Weekly Sentinels* had much to say concerning the red men. He was well acquainted with Friday and his family and did much "harrumphing" on the subject. Like so many frontiersmen, he seemed to feel any retaliation by Indians was *depredation*. However, he also seemed to have a grudging admiration for Friday.

William Marshall Anderson and F.A. Root and W.E. Connelly gave more sketches on the life of Friday, and in more positive form. Rufus Sage touched on his life lightly.

The following sources offered most gratifying help on the background and years of this remarkable man. *Rocky Mountain Journals of William Marshall Anderson*, edited by

Dale L. Morgan and Eleanor T. Harris (San Marino, California: 1967); *Rocky Mountain Life,* by Rufus B. Sage (Lincoln: University of Nebraska, 1982); *Broken Hand,* by Leroy R. Hafen (Lincoln: University of Nebraska, 1981); *People of the Moonshell,* by Nancy M. Peterson (Frederick, Colorado: Renaissance House, 1984); *The Arapaho,* by Alfred L. Knoeber (Lincoln: University of Nebraska, 1983); *The Arapaho,* by Loretta Fowler (New York: Chelsea House, 1989); *Overland Stage to California,* by F.A. Root and W.E. Connelly (Topeka: Privately printed, 1901); and *Annals of Wyoming* (Cheyenne: Wyoming State Historical Society, Spring 1967 and Spring 1974).

Other material on the Arapaho was furnished by Wyoming Indian High School, Ethete, Wyoming.

Early white men did not understand the governing system of the tribal people. They erred when they assumed the chief had full authority. A chief was chosen as spokesmen by informal consensus of their band. Even though some bands had interests in common, each was an independent entity and agreement made with one band was not binding on others.

Charles Erskine Wood, an aide to General O.D. Howard during the Nez Perce war wrote, "I think that in his long career, Joseph cannot accuse the Government of the United States of one single act of justice."

This would seem to serve as a summary for much of the interaction between the tribes and the U.S. government.

✤ MILKMAN MARY

THE RACY YELLOW-WHEELED buggy, drawn by an ugly mare with crooked legs and vicious temper, was a familiar sight on the streets of Laramie for many years. The driver, an elderly lady with work-worn hands and a wrinkled face the old Dutch masters would have loved to paint, was known to all as "Milkman Mary" and more familiarly as "Aunt Mary."

Mary Catherine Erhardt, her husband and two small children came from Bavaria, Germany, and settled on a farm in southeastern Nebraska. Their farm prospered, but family problems and unhappiness followed. Erhardt soon walked away, leaving his young wife and eight-year-old son, Octavian, and baby Dora.

Although she was used to hard work, Mary found that she was unable to operate the farm alone. In 1865, she collected her cattle, loaded a canvas-topped overshot wagon with necessities, hitched up her team of oxen and joined a freighting outfit bound for Denver City, Colorado Territory. The trip took about five weeks.

That year the Sioux and Cheyenne were causing settlers extraordinary difficulties. The tribes swarmed over ranches and isolated farms, killing and burning, attacking frontier towns and destroying many miles of telegraph lines.

45

The wagon train Mary and her children traveled with was attacked, and Indians killed several of the travelers and made off with sixty-five head of cattle. The travelers tightened the wagon corrals and posted heavier night watches to deter the attackers. Mary and her family arrived safely in Denver.

The Erhardts stayed in Denver for two years, supporting themselves by operating a dairy farm. In the spring of 1868, Mary joined a wagon train bound for Cheyenne. The new town promised much for the family. By June, she decided Laramie promised more.

She hired a man to move her outfit and six dairy cows to Laramie. She and the children came over the hill by train. The man left her outfit with the wagon train out by the Big Laramie River. She brought the cattle and wagon into town and, for want of location, pitched her tent in the middle of what proved to be Third Street between South C and D.

She soon bought a lot from the railroad agent and moved her tent from the middle of the street onto the lot, her first roots in Laramie.

When track-layers moved on across the waiting plains and the riff-raff left or were run out of town, Mary took possession of one of the empty frame buildings and had it moved onto her lot. Soon she acquired another shed for her milk cows.

The children herded the cows on the town pasture. Mary peddled milk to customers, dipping the amount from a big pail with a long-handled dipper. She was given the name "Milkman Mary."

She took whatever work she could get. When Noah Wallis and Jack Martin opened a lunchroom, they hired Mary as cook. Daughter Dora soon married Jack Martin, and they went to Montana to live. Octavian is mentioned only in the 1880 census. His age is given as twenty-three, his occupation as stockgrower.

As finances allowed, Mary bought cattle. Her herd grew to three hundred head. She needed space and grass for them. She leased land north of town. There she built a rock house, and a stock barn and pens. She soon moved to her little holding.

In addition to running her own ranch and continuing her milkman rounds, Mary did odd jobs—cleaning house, cooking, and midwifery.

She sold milk at twenty-five cents a quart and cream for two dollars a gallon. In the beginning, she made her rounds on foot, but after moving to the country, she acquired a mean-tempered mare and yellow-wheeled buggy.

According to Burns's *Pioneer Ranches of Wyoming,* Mary "hired no riders. But her brands were known from Medicine Bow to Goshen Hole and from Bate's Hole to the Nebraska line. Wherever or whenever her stock drifted, they were herded back onto their home range by the cowboys. No rustler had the nerve to alter Aunt Mary's brand," so beloved was she.

All riders and passersby who stopped at Mary's home were welcomed with a cheery smile and invited to have a cup of coffee, a slice of cake, a piece of pie or a bit of hot *schnitzkuchen.*

When Dora and Jack Martin moved to Montana, Mary gave up some of her outside work. She didn't give up all social joys, though. Rough and tough though the times, the town and its characters were, many people were still warm and caring.

The courthouse, built in 1872, served as the general gathering place and party hall. Dances held there were a favored jollification, and a good way to raise money for a charity.

"Aunt Mary told of one memorable Fourth of July when the town was assaulted by a raging blizzard," W.S. Ingham wrote in later years. "No one was prepared for such weather and everyone gathered at the courthouse. This way all were accounted for and no one was left cold or in need. The time was spent playing games and dancing.

"When cattle prices took a dive, Mary sold off most of hers and went to raising chickens and turkeys. She may have been the only person to successfully raise turkeys on the Laramie Plains."

After some years Dora and Jack returned to Laramie. They lived with Mary and helped with the activities of her ranch. But Jack was ill and died. He is buried in the Masonic section in Greenhill Cemetery. Dora later married a man named Patch. She died in 1916 and is buried in the Martin plot in Greenhill. There is no mention of Octavian after 1880.

Mary gave up her milk deliveries, but otherwise continued as usual, independent and busy, caring for her place, caring for people and lending a helping hand.

She was past ninety-three when she fell in the corral while doing chores. Her hip was badly injured, possibly broken, for she was unable to move. The woman who had been her companion for two years moved her into the house and telephoned for help. Due to her advanced age, the frail old lady could not recover. She was given the final rites of the Catholic Church and buried beside her daughter in the Martin plot.

The life of this remarkable woman spanned nearly a century, from 1827 to 1921. Her experience covered ocean travel, riding pillion [a passenger sits on a cushion sideways, behind the saddle of the rider], stagecoach and railroad travel. She saw the introduction of telegraph and telephone, electric light and flying machine. She saw the transition from slow-moving ox teams to the thunder of Union Pacific's Overland Limited. She knew the forests and glacier-dressed mountains of German Bavaria, the gentle midlands of America, the rolling prairies of Nebraska and the awesome beauty of the Laramie Plains.

This kindly woman knew no stranger, her heart and hand were open to all, and few ill words were ever spoken of her.

∞

BIBLIOGRAPHICAL ESSAY. Sources for Mary's story were the *Laramie Sentinel* and the *Laramie Boomerang* newspapers; the book *Wyoming Pioneer Ranches* by Burns, Gillespie and Richardson (Laramie: Top of the World Press, 1957); Albany County records; Greenhill Cemetery records and the 1880 census.

◇◇◇ ◇◇◇ ◇◇◇ ◇◇◇ ◇◇◇ ◇◇◇ ◇◇◇ ◇◇◇ ◇◇◇ ◇◇◇ ◇◇◇ ◇◇◇ ◇◇◇ ◇◇◇ ◇◇◇

FROM THE *LARAMIE DAILY BOOMERANG*
MARCH, 1895

THE PERILS OF BICYCLE RIDING BECAME APPARENT WHEN A YOUNG LADY WAS DISCOVERED ON SECOND STREET CAUGHT IN THE COILS OF HER BIKE. HER SKIRTS WERE SO WOUND UP IN THE REAR SPROCKET THAT SHE HAD TO REMOVE THEM. THE ASSISTANCE OF A GENTLEMAN WAS REQUIRED TO CARRY HER BIKE HOME.

MORAL: WEAR BLOOMERS.

◇◇◇ ◇◇◇ ◇◇◇ ◇◇◇ ◇◇◇ ◇◇◇ ◇◇◇ ◇◇◇ ◇◇◇ ◇◇◇ ◇◇◇ ◇◇◇ ◇◇◇ ◇◇◇ ◇◇◇

✤ A Melancholy Love Story

T HEY WERE AN attractive couple on the dance floor at the Fort Sanders cotillions—Philip Mandel with his dark coloring and carefully-groomed beard, and Jane Alexander, the fair young widow from Virginia.

Mandel operated a stage station on the Denver-Salt Lake route, which later became Holladay's Overland Stage Line. When the Sixth Dakota Legislative Assembly created counties in the Wyoming District, they named Philip Mandel as one of the three commissioners of Laramie County with Fort Sanders as county seat.

The meetings of the commissioners accounted for Mandel's frequent presence at the fort and presented opportunity for him to see the fair Scottish woman.

Jane Alexander, or Jennie as she was better known, had been influenced by her father Major Ronald Campbell, a military engineer, to marry Major John Alexander of the U.S. Army.

Scarcely had their honeymoon ended when Major Alexander became ill and died in a southern city. Shortly after his death, their son John was born. When war erupted between the states, Jennie enlisted as a nurse in the Confederate Army and served until peace was declared. With a contingent of soldiers, Jennie and little Johnnie came West to Fort Sanders in 1867.

The fort hospital was not complete, although there was a fairly competent medical service. Dr. J.H. Finfrock was transferred from the abandoned Fort Halleck to the new fort and welcomed Jennie's service as a nurse.

Mandel and Jennie at once became "a recognized pair." They were married January 24, 1871. They lived on the Mandel ranch. Although Indian dangers were greatly reduced by 1871, Philip was concerned for the safety of his bride and her son. They were frequently in town.

In July 1872, eleven-year-old Johnnie, who was fascinated by trains and trainmen, lost his right arm under the railroad cars. Shock, loss of blood, and possibly gangrene caused his death three weeks later.

In January 1874, Jennie and Philip named their newborn son Louis Philip. He lived only six months. The cause of death was not given. Even though she was a nurse, Jennie could not save the baby.

She could not become truly accustomed to the primitive life on their ranch, and in her grief, she may have blamed this and their isolation as causes of their baby's death.

Mandel himself had become calloused by frontier hardship, but wanted to please his beloved Jennie and wanted another son. He bought lots in Laramie City in 1875 and built a substantial brick house at the corner of Fourth and South C (Garfield), now the site of Pacific Power and Light.

So the young Mandels had a fine town house and their ranch home in the beautiful Little Laramie River Valley.

In the spring of 1878, Mandel sold part of his holdings to Galusha B. Grow for $29,500. In spite of his love for Jennie, Philip could not resist the lure of the far country. In the winter of 1878, he formed a partnership with James Bannon and set up a grocery, grain and feed store in the northern wilderness on the Big Goose Creek not far from the present site of Sheridan.

The northern part of the territory was still staggering from the Indian battles of 1876, and while settlers were steadily drifting into the area, the Mandel-Bannon business was not a success. They returned to Laramie and a short while later built a brick block building with an iron front at the corner of Second and Garfield.

The Mandel daughters were born in their Garfield Street home, Katherine in September 1881, and Margaret in 1886.

The family spent summers on their Little Laramie ranch, feeling safer with each passing year and the apparent resolution of Indian problems. But, like all love stories, the Mandels' was not always idyllic.

Philip began spending more and more time in the country, increasingly reverting to the careless habits of his earlier frontier life, and for long stretches at a time, increasingly indifferent to his family and their needs.

Jennie assumed nursing duties from time to time at the private hospital operated by Mrs. C.N. Northrup on North Fourth Street. In 1892, she became afflicted by an "undisclosed, incurable disease."

Later when both girls were married with families, Jennie traveled alone to Denver for the medical treatment not available in Laramie. The trips, plus coping with her illness and her husband's indifference, became difficult for Jennie to bear.

In August 1905, Jennie sued Philip for maintenance. He was "ordered to contribute forty dollars per month for her support plus one hundred and fifty dollars for medical expenses." The newspapers reported they had lived apart for some time.

Jennie could no longer work at the hospital. Lonely, discouraged and rejected, she moved to Denver. She died in Mercy Hospital on June 25, 1907, and was buried in Denver.

Philip, then age seventy-three, remained for a time on the ranch. Increasingly forgetful and frail, he was at last persuaded to move to town. He lived with daughter Katherine Lasher and her two children at 412 Grand Avenue. He spent time off and on at the Northrup Hospital.

His guardian, with power-of-attorney, wrote checks against Mandel's account—with apparent disregard for the old frontiersman or his heirs. Cash reserves were sadly depleted, and Philip Mandel, once considered well-to-do, was reduced almost to a poor-house state.

On the evening of October 21, 1917, Philip Mandel expressed a deep longing to pay a visit to the old ranch. Katherine apparently promised to fulfill his wish, but when she went to call him the next morning, she discovered he had died in his sleep. He was eighty-three.

∞

BIBLIOGRAPHICAL ESSAY. Sources for this love story were the previously cited *Pioneer Ranches of Wyoming;* I.S. Bartlett's *History of Wyoming* (Chicago: S.J. Clarke Publishing, 1918)*; Annals of Wyoming* (Spring 1961); Albany County records; Greenhill Cemetery records; and newspapers, including the *Laramie Daily* and *Weekly Sentinel, Republican* and *Boomerang,* and the *Rocky Mountain News.*

❦ WOES OF WILLIAM

*"If ever there was a poor, persecuted man, that man
is William Crout...a proverb says in all man's troubles...
there is a woman at the bottom, but in Crout's case
there's at least a dozen....
He does not claim to have but two, legitimate wives now...."*
Laramie Daily Sentinel
July 22, 1875

YES, WILLIAM CROUT was a marryin' man. His first venture was in February 1855, in Kent County, Michigan, to
Melissa A. Bryant. She apparently was the mother of
their children.

William was a persevering, energetic man. He first saw
the Laramie Plains in 1852 on his way to California. His
obituary states he spent from 1852 to 1857 in California,
Oregon and the Pacific region. When did he have time to
wed, back in Michigan? Between 1855 and 1861 he fathered
several children. The youngest son, David Frank was born
October 14, 1861.

William was a frontiersman, too, and "a very agreeable
conversationalist." It is possible for tellers of tales to forget
dates—or mix them up—and this could have been a problem
for William, forgetting dates.

∞ William Crout added on to the Frontier Hotel during the time that he owned it. (Beery Collection)

Public records, then, show his first marriage in February 1855 in Michigan. The family arrived in Laramie City, according to city history, in 1868. William helped build Fort Sanders (1867) and cut hay for the Holladay Stage Line horses. Then William bought the first building that was erected in the new Laramie City—the Frontier Hotel. The family moved into town in 1869.

This flat, treeless grassland, so forlorn, surrounded by mountains that by turn loomed near or crouched low, mysterious in blue haze, was not home to Melissa.

She longed for the known forest of Michigan. So she left. As did Wife Number two, also a native of Michigan. And Number three left, but she may merely have been a housekeeper. After all, there was the Frontier Hotel to look after and the Crout children, who were by now teenagers.

William was patient and gracious and bore no grudges against his women. There were more housekeepers where those came from. But he apparently gave up on wooing women from Michigan. His next choice was a lady with a Laramie background.

In that sparkling 1875 spoof of William's marital ventures in the *Laramie Daily Sentinel,* the editor, J.H. Hayford, opines:

"We believe he does not claim to have but two legitimate wives now, in this city.... Occasionally some charitable individual will take one off his hands for a time...but bad pennies sooner or later always return to vex his righteous soul from day to day. Women are so unreasonable...."

According to the newspaper, Crout had replaced one of these "unreasonable women" when the deserter returned claiming her rightful place as wife and homemaker.

"Crout, who is of a forgiving turn of mind, took the repentant spouse back to his bed and board and sent number 10 away to cool," the newspaper jibed gleefully. "But instead of cooling, she fermented and finally turned to Sour Crout."

The case went to court; Sour Crout resolved to have a trial of right of property.

Judge Pease brought up the matter of the value of property and even suggested Solomon's decision—cutting Crout into halves and letting the women play a game of seven-up for choice of halves.

But Attorney Bramel "brought up the criminal features of the case and poor Crout was bound over on charges of adultery, fornication and all manner of evil concupiscence...."

It turned out all right, though. William obtained a divorce and was legally wed to Mary Ann. She stayed with him two years, and Will again resorted to his form. He placed a notice in the *Sentinel:* "Whereas my wife, Mary Ann (or name applying to my wife) has left my bed and board without any just cause or provocation, I will pay no bills of her contracting."

Another divorce and Crout was free again.

*

All Will's troubles were not with his own wives, which were fewer *of record* than the newspaper hinted at.

Crout owned the Frontier Hotel and had added a new frame section, a three-story affair that could accommodate one hundred guests, the newspaper reported.

He leased the bar, which was in the basement, and the hotel itself, sometimes to the same lessee. More often the leases were separate. In 1877, Ted Bath ran the bar. Coolbroth and a partner out of Cheyenne had the hotel portion. The partner soon pulled out. A few weeks later Coolbroth informed Crout he wanted out of the lease, too. Crout blew up.

The pair were exchanging loud what-fors with each other when Mrs. Lincoln, a guest, stepped into the fray.

The lady claimed a family relationship with Coolbroth and had been stopping at the hotel for two or three months, giving piano lessons and lessons in language.

Crout didn't care for her intrusion and gave her a lesson in language, uttering "approbious epithets referring to her character."

Coolbroth took umbrage and wired the lady's husband in Cheyenne, "Wife's honor at stake. Will you vindicate or shall I?" Lincoln replied "I'll come."

He did.

While the three talked in the hotel parlor, William emerged from the basement and crossed the yard to his private residence. Out the two men ran, Lincoln with a gun. He fired at Crout.

Will fell, shot in the ankle. But he got up and ran to his

own door. The Cheyenne man shot again, striking Crout in the right thigh, narrowly missing the femoral artery.

Sheriff Dan Nottage arrived quickly, arrested the three Cheyenne people and put them in the city jail to cool off. The next day Mrs. Lincoln shook the dust of Laramie from her feet and returned to Cheyenne by train.

Crout spent three weeks in the hospital and moved about carefully with a cane when released. His seating arrangement was somewhat altered too, for a number of months.

Coolbroth was released from the hotel lease. He and Lincoln paid Crout for their impulsive actions, plus medical and hospital bills for William. They henceforth stayed east of old Sherman Hill.

But William Crout now had to pay $34.05 in fines to Judge Bill Nye's court for the mouthful of obscenities he had spat at the lady from Cheyenne. Not the first or last fine he paid for free speech, however.

Crout was now free of Mary Ann, but he soon found another. This Mary, who remains a mystery except in the 1880 census which states her age as 42, stayed with William until February 2, 1882. She left and was still gone on April 7, 1883, when Will filed yet another petition for divorce on grounds of desertion.

This Mary took with her about five hundred dollars worth of linens and household furnishings, which could have been hers in the first place.

A witness at the hearings was Mrs. Elizabeth Casteel, who acted as housekeeper after Mary II left.

The divorce was granted, and on May 19, 1883, Elizabeth and William were married.

Early the year before Crout had sold the four lots on which the old Frontier Hotel complex stood. He had always taken on odd-jobbing, leaving his lessees to run the hotel works.

He won the contract to move 30,363 cubic yards of Wyoming dirt to create the Pioneer Canal. Also, with his son-in-law Davis he put up a number of houses and other buildings in town. Among his efforts was the Skating Rink for Johnnie (Oyster-House) Dimmit on Third Street. It later became Mannerchor Hall.

Crout and Elizabeth left Laramie when those contracts were fulfilled and moved to a ranch on the upper North Platte Valley where his youngest son David Frank had holdings.

Then he lost Elizabeth, this time to a Higher Court. She died in the Spring of 1888, and he was again alone.

But he knew what to do.

In January, 1889, the *Sentinel* reported: "Crout is back in town and trying to snore the roof off the Kuster House.... The building still stands, although it is shaky."

Will didn't stay long enough to snore the hotel down. On February 23, 1889, he married Mrs. Elizabeth Bechtold.

How clever was Will! Most of his marriage arrangements occurred in the same months, so it wasn't too difficult to recall an anniversary. And in later years he even chose wives with like names, so if he talked in his sleep—.

William died in 1894, a respected pioneer, full of years and probably quite wise.

∞

BIBLIOGRAPHICAL ESSAY. There are many sources for the story on William Crout. First and most frequent references were found in Laramie's *Daily* and *Weekly Sentinels*.

District Court Number two records supplied material on his divorces as well as various legal problems that the old pioneer faced, most of which are omitted from this story.

Albany County marriage records provide marriage information except when the ceremony occurred out of state. Then newspaper items are cited.

Pioneer Ranches of Wyoming, previously cited, gave information concerning Crout's son David. *Annals of Wyoming* mentions Crout in stories of other subjects and people.

The story of the *Frontier Index,* the "sassy little sheet" that moved west with the construction of the Union Pacific Railroad, relating news and occurrences along the way, was instrumental in looking into the history of Crout, although the paper itself never mentions the man, nor did its publishers ever hear of him. The *Index* was gone before Crout bought the hotel.

THE FIRST BALLOTING IN LARAMIE CITY WAS IN 1870 AT THE LARAMIE CITY COURTHOUSE, WHICH WAS THE OLD NATIONAL THEATRE/BLUE FRONT BUILDING, MRS. LOUISA SWAIN, AGE 80 PLUS, CAST THE FIRST BALLOT. THE APRON SHE WORE WAS SOLD AT AUCTION A FEW WEEKS LATER AND WAS PURCHASED BY A MAN FROM WASHINGTON FOR TEN DOLLARS. IT IS NOT KNOWN IF HE WAS FROM WASHINGTON STATE OR WASHINGTON, D.C. HE SAID LATER HE WOULD HAVE GONE AS HIGH AS FIFTY DOLLARS TO OWN THAT APRON BELONGING TO THE WORLD'S FIRST WOMAN VOTER.

❧ FRONT STREET COURTHOUSE

T HE STORY OF LARAMIE City's first courthouse on Front Street stretches over seventy-five years. The building first served as a notorious deadfall operated by murderers, later as a sleazy business used as a courtroom when needed, and most recently as a respectable business establishment.

In those six months of Laramie's roaring beginning, the dive was run by the Asa Moore-Sam Dugan gang, as was the whole town. When their careers were abruptly ended by a rope in the hands of vigilantes in October 1868, their low, log building near the corner of present-day Garfield and First Streets was left vacant.

Irish railroader Ed Shaughnessey quickly moved in, appropriated the equipment and ran a saloon, gambling, and vaudeville house which he called the National Theatre. No one was killed and no bodies were added under the dirt floor while he ran the joint. When he left town in early spring of 1869 with his vaudeville actress wife Fanny Garretson, Faro dealer Paul Fuhr took over.

In July, eighteen-year-old business-wise Ulrike Trabing bought the land from the Union Pacific Railroad company and the saloon-gambling building from Paul Fuhr. She and her husband, August, painted the front of their National Theatre a brilliant blue. In time, it became known as the "Blue

∞ The portion of the building under the words "The Laramie" was the first courthouse. (Beery Collection)

Front" and the National Theatre title was forgotten.

Vaudeville entertainment continued with many unknown performers and a few better knowns such as Eddie Foy and the fiery Lola Montez. August Trabing was fond of relating how he often "trod the boards" of that Front Street stage.

When the Trabings moved to Medicine Bow to operate their prospering freighting and store-provisions business, Mrs. Trabing leased the National Theatre to their bartender George Weiske.

Part of Weiske's rent was to "raise the walls four feet, put on a new substantial roof (to replace the canvas one) and lay a new floor…" (to cover the dirt floor that had so conveniently served the Moore gang as a burial ground).

The lease ran from December 6, 1869, to December 6, 1870. In March 1870, the saloon was rented by the county to serve as courtroom for the court session when the famous "first mixed jury" was impanelled. It was the first jury in the world to seat both men and women.

Many coarse jokes circulated about women jurors. Several of the women planned to beg off, partly because of the jokes, partly because of the newness of the idea, and partly because of the location. No *lady ever* went to Front Street.

Judge John H. Howe, "a man of good ability," sympathized with them, but told the ladies there was "not the slightest impropriety in any lady occupying a position" on the panel. They would be given respect and protection and the thanks of the public for their work.

With ladies on the jury, a definite air of respect for the law was restored. Card and dice games were suspended, feet were kept on the floor instead of on nearby chairs, drinking and smoking were also suspended and chewing was done more circumspectly, making use of spittoons.

That mixed jury brought congratulations from many world figures and heads of state. At the end of the court session, it was conceded that the "law had been enforced and equal, impartial, exact justice meted out to all in every instance" and that the women had "acquitted themselves with dignity and rendered verdicts befitting the occasion" which confounded the most skeptical of chin-pullers.

When Weiske's lease expired, the Trabings leased their blue-painted National Theatre to Charlie Kuster for a year. The next session of court met again in the saloon, and Kuster received seventy-five dollars for rent of the place.

The stigma of doing jury duty in a grogshop-courtroom on Laramie's notorious Front Street did not stain reputations thereafter, for the county's new courthouse was completed in time for 1872 hearings.

The saloon did not stand empty, however. It continued to dispense liquid cheer until Trabing stocked and opened it as a grocery store, thus lending dignity to the once-maligned place. Until 1883 the Blue Front, as it was now referred to, was one of Trabing's grocery and outfitting stores. When Trabing's big new store opened on Second Street the old grogshop became their warehouse. The Blue Front logo continued to serve as Trabing's Laramie symbol.

After the great Trabing fire of 1895 and the subsequent bankruptcy proceedings, the building was later owned by the Laramie Grocery Company. Then the one-time dive settled into near-oblivion.

As a warehouse, the building lost all personality and public attention. Then in 1912 Grace Raymond Hebard, prominent in University of Wyoming academic circles, aroused interest in the old landmark and caused a bronze plaque to be placed on the wall of the building.

Rumors that it was a place for amative adventure contain no logic. With kerosene, tools, baled hay and grocery items stored in the original building as well as in the addition on the south side, all behind locked doors, there was no way for anyone to get inside. Besides, the real incentive for dalliance stood next door to the north at Minnie Ford's parlor-house.

The one-time house of vice, one-time courtroom, long since covered over with galvanized tin, was razed in the 1940s, thus bringing to a close one special bit of history of Laramie's early days.

Bad luck dogged many of those associated with that famous building.

Asa Moore, Con Wager and Big Ed Wilson were hanged in Laramie after their six-month spree of ruling the town. One of the gang who escaped that October cleanup was Sam Dugan. He was hanged a few years later in Colorado.

Ed Shaughnessey was shot at Deadwood, South Dakota, in a quarrel with his ex-wife's lover. Fanny Garretson went to Dodge City after being run out of Sidney, Nebraska, and was shot in a saloon brawl.

Paul Fuhr escaped the Meeker massacre only to die poorly in Oregon.

Ulrike and August Trabing were divorced. Gus later went bankrupt after the disastrous fire. Ulrike made money with her divorce settlement, re-married and went to Omaha to live. August's brother, Charles Trabing, died of blood-poisoning from a scratch by a rusty nail.

H.H. Richards, a clerk at the Blue Front, and his wife Harriett divorced after a rousing quarrel. He never re-married. She did.

One of Trabing's imaginative ads read: "O great is Trabing, and Stryker is his Profit." J.W. Stryker, Blue Front clerk and later mortician, lost his wife to incurable illness.

Even a mule associated with the building found public disgrace. According to newspaper man Bill Nye, the mule that walked into Trabing's newly dug basement, forgetting his barn no longer stood there, had to endure great embarrassment and the horse laugh of the town.

A plaque commemorates the site of that Front Street Courthouse where the world-famous mixed jury served—but has long marked the wrong site.

∞

BIBLIOGRAPHICAL ESSAY. Reference is made in the old Laramie *Sentinel* to the National Theater as scene of the first court session in Laramie City. My research of land records in the office of the Albany County Clerk has revealed ownership—and the absence thereof after the exodus of the tough element in 1868.

Other references were found in the County Commissioner's Book of Proceedings, showing payment of rent for the building during court sessions.

Other references refer to the three hoodlums hanged on October 18, 1868. They were "taken from their dead-fall and hanged from a pole (or a summer-beam or a rafter, depending on where the item is found) at an unfinished log cabin over on Second Street." My research, and reference to early maps of the town, places the cabin in question at the corner of Third and Kearney.

The saloon-vaudeville theater (later store) was called the Tin-plate Restaurant in one item.This probably was during the Shaughnessey ownership.

A later item gave the measurement of the building as forty feet by forty feet. This fits later descriptions when the Tra-bings added to the east end of the building and turned it into the famous Blue Front store.

✠ JUDGE AND JURY

IN 1869, JOHN W. Kingman of New Hampshire was appointed Associate Chief Justice of the Supreme Court of Wyoming Territory by President Ulysses S. Grant. He came to the wilderness in time to participate in one of the world-shaking events of western history—allowing women the privilege of serving on trial juries.

All new territorial officers arrived in the new territory of Wyoming at about the same time, so they set about organizing the government and the courts.

"We found a horrible condition," Judge Kingman later wrote. "Apparently the worst men and women who fled from the border states and elsewhere for various reasons seemed to dominate the society here. The courts were powerless to enforce common criminal laws even in cases of high crimes. A common remark heard in the jury room was, 'One man is dead, why do you want to kill another one?'"

This viewpoint was shared in many frontier courtrooms, it seems. The usual approach of a jury was "self-defense" or "Aw, he didn't do no harm—let 'im go."

Jurors played cards, rolled dice and continued their smoking, tobacco-chewing and spitting and sprawled about lazily during court proceedings. There was no such thing as respect for the Court.

Kingman relates his introduction to the new legislature thus: "The members were paid by the United States Government but they voted themselves a large additional salary to be paid out of Territorial funds. Application was made to prevent this steal. The Chief Justice was absent and I was acting in his place. There was a great deal of grumbling, but the injunction was never appealed from or revoked...."

Dr. T. A. Larson, Professor Emeritus of History at the University of Wyoming, gives the following information: "Regular pay for Legislators was four dollars per day. They voted themselves an additional six dollars per day for regular members and twelve dollars for presiding officers...."

Governor Campbell agreed with Kingman, but was overridden by the legislators. The law was later nullified and a set fee approved.

Kingman found some of the attorneys "most wretched characters." He disbarred two of them and sent two others to prison for thirty days each. These characters "left the Territory," he stated, "and never returned."

The enfranchisement giving women equal rights with men was passed by the first Legislature after much debate. The action was approved, not so much from conviction that it was a good thing, but more because there was a general feeling that the Governor would veto the bill.

Kingman relates that Governor Campbell was inclined to do so, but that Kingman and Judge Howe talked with him one night long past midnight and finally convinced him to sign it.

There was much bitter feeling against the bill, and it was apparent at the first session of the District Court after the act was passed.

This session of court was held in Laramie City in March 1870, with Judge Howe presiding.

To forestall ridicule and trouble, Kingman relates, the Judge "summoned nearly all the respectable women in the city as jurors making both petit and grand juries largely composed of women."

Many of the husbands were furious and interpreted it as an insult and an outrage. They made threats of violence and there was much loud and dangerous talk. Some men even declared their wives need never come home if they served on a jury.

The two judges conferred and agreed that any woman had the right to sit as a juror and should not be driven out unless she chose to leave. A few women asked to be excused before the first court met.

The furor was much more intense than for any previous trial, and the courtroom was jam-packed. Some came out of curiosity, others to see the fun, but most were seething with anger. The publicity brought reporters from far away; newspaper reports and accompanying cartoons were most uncomplimentary.

On the crucial morning, the selected women were all there in obedience to the summons.

Judge Howe had asked Judge Kingman to sit with him and assist in the proceedings. Judge Howe announced to the court and to the women that this was a new and unusual affair, and he would not require any woman to serve on any jury against her will. But for those who chose to exercise the *rights given her by law*, the full power of the law would protect her against insult and/or interference either in the courtroom, or in the streets, or *in her own home*. The power of the law and Court would visit the most extreme punishment upon transgressors.

Judge Kingman then reminded the impanelled persons of the previous laxity of enforcement of criminal laws and that the jurors to date had been unwilling to convict those plainly guilty.

"We believe this may be remedied if intelligent, moral and brave women will come forward and exercise these new powers that are now placed in your hands. We believe you are more deeply interested in sustaining honest and vigorous enforcement of the laws and [will] help us to protect this young society being formed on this frontier."

Judge Howe then stated again that any woman who wished to be excused need only ask, but he hoped they would remain and serve. And Judge Kingman related, "To the surprise of nearly everyone, they all chose to remain."

Attorney Stephan W. Downey furiously denounced the panel as illegal because it was not composed of male citizens. W.R. Steele and T.J. Street argued in favor of the mixed panel, and the judges upheld them.

Court records of March 7, 1870, show fifteen names impanelled as Grand Jurors: Frederick Laycock, J.W. Teats, Amelia Hatcher, W.H. Harlow, Louis Miller, M.A. Hance, Mrs. G.F. Hilton, W.S. Bramel, Charles Bussard, Charles Hutton, Eliza Stewart, Mary Mackle, Sarah W. Pease, B.C. Dunton, and George W. Lancaster. Twelve persons comprised the jury with three to act as alternates. Laycock was appointed Court Foreman of the Grand Jury.

This court sat for three weeks and heard several cases of murder, as well as cases of horse and cattle stealing and illegal branding of livestock.

The following women were called on the first Petit Jury: Retta Burnham, Nellie Hazen, Mary Wilcox, Mary L. Flynn, Mrs. I.M. Hartsough, Lizzie A. Spooner and Jennie Ivinson. Mary Flynn, Lizzie Spooner and Jennie Ivinson asked to be excused.

Those women who served on that historic first mixed jury conducted themselves in a highly responsible and exemplary manner and even inspired the jurymen to respectful courtroom conduct.

For all the teeth-gnashing and frothing at the mouth generated in the beginning, it was later conceded that the verdicts handed down were thoughtful and just. The presence of women jurors had resulted in more impartial and honest verdicts than those delivered by any previous juries.

Frequent requests entered later by law-breakers for a change of venue were said to be from "fear of those women jurors."

This new and unusual exercise in court procedure attracted all the attention that the legislators thought it would, but for different reasons.

Telegrams, letters and messages from around the world arrived to congratulate this fledgling territory on its forward-looking, open-mindedness in accepting women as partners, equal to men. This flood of recognition brought about a new outlook and much back-patting among the men of the territory, and they quickly adopted the motto: Wyoming, the EQUALITY STATE.

∞

BIBLIOGRAPHICAL ESSAY. Judge John W. Kingman's article in *Annals of Wyoming,* (Vol. 14, No. 3) furnished substantial material for this chapter.

Also consulted was Dr. T.A. Larson's *History of Wyoming,* (Lincoln: University of Nebraska, 1965) concerning the first Territorial Legislature.

Albany County Court Records were used.

Dr. Grace Raymond Hebard's "The First Woman Jury" republished by Laramie Graphics from a 1913 volume of the *Journal of American History* was another source.

The long term effects of this experiment are apparent. In March 10, 1883, *Laramie Daily Boomerang* in an item noted, "Even Cheyenne is calling for women on juries!"

The memoirs of pioneer Michael Arthur Carroll, whose suit against horse thieves was one of the first cases heard by the mixed jury, was also consulted.

🎷 THE LADY BAILIFF

THE WORLD'S FIRST lady court bailiff of record was Martha Symons-Bois, an Englishwoman of "large proportions and commanding presence." She served the Laramie City, Wyoming, court.

Pictures show her as having dark hair, a firm mouth and square, determined jaw, relieved by a deep dimple in her chin.

When the first mixed Grand Jury heard testimony in a murder case and, after deliberating all day, failed to reach a decision by nightfall, rooms were engaged for the panel at the Union Pacific Hotel, one for men and one for women jurors.

The two bailiffs herded the group up First Street from the courtroom in the National Theatre and posted themselves outside the hotel room door. The name of the man bailiff has not been recorded, but Martha Symons-Bois served as the bailiff guarding the door of the ladies' chamber.

Given such a formidable guard before the jury door, it must have been quite plain that no jeers, harassment or shenanigans would be tolerated.

In 1870, names of jurors were not drawn. Selection was made by the sheriff of the county. N.K. Boswell was sheriff of Albany County. He personally made the selections and called on those chosen.

Symons-Bois was born Martha Uren in 1830 in England,

but her parents sailed to North America when she was only a few weeks old. They settled in Wisconsin. Martha was first married October 16, 1861, to John Symons. They had two sons, John H. and James, and a daughter who died in infancy. Sometime after the death of Mr. Symons, Martha married Jeremiah Bois, a divorced man with one son, Curtis.

The three boys did not get along well, and Curtis disliked the lady who took his mother's place. It was not a serene household.

The family headed westward while the Union Pacific Railroad construction was getting underway at Omaha, Nebraska Territory. They stopped for a time at old Fort Kearney and operated a hotel in a meanly-constructed building in Dobietown. [Dobietown was a shack-town not related to Fort Kearney in any way. It was said to be a "low-down collection of buildings and joints."] When the rails reached that place, the Boises quit the hotel business and ran a boarding house for the railroaders instead. It proved to be a lucrative business, so when construction moved westward, the Bois family did too, going from camp to camp feeding the workmen in their tent eating-house.

The long winter of 1866 halted construction of the railroad at North Platte Station. Martha and Jeremiah enjoyed a thriving business in the riverside town. Friendships formed there during that rigorous winter later affected their decision to settle in Laramie.

When work resumed in the spring, the Boises followed. The hectic days at Julesburg, the boisterous camp-life and rough, dirty workmen fazed them not at all. They were pleased their culinary efforts were appreciated.

Martha and Jeremiah Bois, with their three squabbling boys, arrived in Laramie City in their prairie schooner on May 9, 1868, the day before the first train did.

∞ Martha Symons-Bois, the first lady bailiff, was a woman of commanding presence. (Drawing by B.J. Durr based on a photo)

"The town was a collection of tents then," Martha recalled in later years. "We lived in a tent all that first year. By the next year we occupied a frame house on Centre Street [Centre is now University] back of Mr. Bois's furniture and undertaking business. The Methodist Episcopal Church was built that year across the street east of us at the corner of Second and Centre. Mr. Bois and George Fox worked to obtain lots from the railroad company for the church building. They helped with the formal organization and both were members of the first Board of Trustees."

Martha kept busy trying to tame the quarrelsome boys, helping her husband in his undertaking business and operating her boarding house. The work at the undertaking parlors came about because help could seldom be found to lay out and prepare a corpse for burial, and there were many in those days. It was even difficult to find a man to drive the hearse, and Martha was often forced to take over that task, as well.

Curtis Bois returned to his mother in Iowa after a few years, and the household settled into a quieter routine. The boarding house took much time. The boarders were all working men with "outdoor appetites." Martha, in later years, expressed enthusiasm for so many "perfectly splendid men" with whom she came in contact in all phases of her work.

One of the surprises of her frontier experiences was having two of her boarders hanged by the Vigilance Committee in the October 1868 cleanup of the town. These two men were Con Wager and Big Ed Wilson.

Martha didn't mention if the two executed boarders were included in her list of "perfectly splendid men."

The stint as bailiff was Martha's only venture in holding public office. W.E. Chaplin related that "as bailiff of Judge Howe's court there appears to be nothing to indicate that Mrs. Bois was not a good and worthy officer."

Without doubt this woman was well-chosen by Sheriff Boswell to act as bailiff of the court.

∞

BIBLIOGRAPHICAL ESSAY. Sources for this chapter are Grace Raymond Hebard's pamphlet on "The First Woman Jury," previously cited.

Reminiscences of W.E. Chaplin's early days in Laramie published in the *Laramie Republican* in the 1940s was helpful. The *Laramie Sentinel* listed jurors serving on Grand and Petit Juries in 1870 and 1871. The Albany County Commissioners' Proceedings (Book I) provided additional information.

✣ Mrs. Jackson K. Brown

S HE CAME FROM County Clare, Ireland, in 1858. Her
name was Diana Harran. She was sixteen.

Diana, her mother Bridgit, brother Richard and sister
Alice were scheduled to ship out for America—all goods
aboard, their passage cleared, goodbyes said, then Alice
became ill of fever. She died the night before the ship was to
sail, so the Harrans made the heartbreaking decision to leave
her burial and last rites to relatives and friends, for the ship
would not wait.

After their arrival in New York, through the good offices
of Irish emigrants in the city, Richard found work, and it
seemed the new move was blessed. They loved their new
country. Even with the scorn poured upon the Irish emigrants
at that period in history, they did not cry small. They worked,
they sang, they danced, and they loved their new country and
upheld its laws. They did not insist on special treatment.

When war erupted between the states, Richard enlisted
with the Army of the North. And when peace was declared
the family found themselves in Rolla, Missouri.

Young Harran worked with the transportation department
of the Union Army as bull-whacker. Jackson K. Brown was
wagonmaster. Their route was along the military road known

as the "Old Wire Road," where a telegraph line had been strung between Rolla and Fort Smith, Arkansas, in 1862.

When Jackson K., then 38, and the pretty, vivacious Diana met it didn't take long for them to decide to wed. Diana was only twenty, but the wide difference in age was shrugged off. After all, age mattered little; it was what you were and what you could do that counted.

Jackson Brown, a part of the early contingent on the site of Fort Sanders in Dakota Territory, was attached to the command of Major Belcher, but as a civilian. Young Harran stayed with Brown as drover.

Belcher was assigned the task of transferring buildings from old Fort Halleck, miles away at the northern toe of Elk Mountain, to use in establishing the new fort at the southern end of the Laramie Plains. Even with sawmills and the most modern equipment, this fort was a primitive affair.

Personnel were housed mostly in tent-houses, and when the frame and log buildings were erected, often the tents were more comfortable. Floors were left with open knot-holes, walls were unsealed against the sweeping winds, windows were often loosely fitted, and no trees existed anywhere to give shade against a brilliant sun.

Civilians, of course, could arrange for their own housing. Easy enough, for logs were piled along the banks of the Big Laramie River to sell to any buyer or to be made into railroad ties.

Brown soon had a cabin ready for his family, and Diana, their two small daughters and her mother Bridgit arrived in Cheyenne in 1867 where the railroad ended. Jackson met them there with an army ambulance and brought them to their new home at the fort on the wide, wind-scoured Laramie Plains.

Probably the first reaction of all newcomers to these great grasslands, stretching from horizon to horizon in awesome but frightening beauty, was dismay. Miles of long, waving grass flowed in every direction. On three sides, hemming in the great hanging valley, arose mountains, hovering in the distance, blue with evening mysteries, towering and snow covered, sometimes seeming to creep close under a tender blue sky to give a sense of comfort and welcome to newcomers.

To Irish Diana and her mother, accustomed to the moist greenery of Ireland, it must have seemed daunting. They were not long in transplanting wild flowers and the unfamiliar cactus with its waxy flowers to their cabin yard. It took only one warning to the children to stay away from the cactus. They even became accustomed to the wild animals that ventured near the fort, not yet afraid of human beings. They became accustomed to seeing "tame" Indians around the fort.

The townsite of the future Laramie City was then laid out. A clutch of early-comers were already squatting on the grounds. No one felt completely isolated from civilization. Daily emigrant trains arrived from the East, and discouraged travelers returning to their homes passed through from the West. Some stopped at the new town-site for work was plentiful. It was a bustling, noisy community.

Jackson acquired an eighty-acre tract of land on the bare plain just north of the fort limits and moved his cabin from the fort to their new holding. Little Jackson Brown was born in the fort hospital in 1869. With the desired son to carry on the Brown name, their family was complete.

That fall Jackson left the army employ and began cultivating the small farm. He set up a business trading well-fed, rested horses and oxen to travelers for their travel-worn, footsore critters. He did well until his health began to fail. Exposure to the fretful weather of the trail had brought on rheumatism and a heart condition that often kept him abed.

Diana, keen-eyed and clever, with memories of the

shaggy Irish ponies, quickly learned the ways of a good trader from her husband. When Jackson was obliged to take to his bed, Diana served as an excellent substitute. They prospered.

Few ways were open to a woman of that era to make a living—either she had to become cook or washerwoman for some household or a doxy. When Jackson died Diana had the background, knowledge and confidence to continue with the family enterprise.

Her livestock grazed on the free range near the fort and town. Daughters Anna and Josephine became daring and confident horseback riders so were often given the task of herding to keep their stock within safe limits. Indians called the cattle "whoa-haws" after the yells the bullwhackers made to the oxen. They tended to ignore the cattle even as food, but they had a good eye and long reach when it came to mules and horses.

Surprisingly for a woman, Diana did well. A number of the Englishmen who were drawn by the promise of the broad plains relied on Diana for the best livestock to supply their ranges. Most of them, however, imported blooded stock which was crossbred with the best of what Diana selected to sell.

She got along well with her neighbors, even the feisty German J.J. Fein. They were much alike, and even joined in a lawsuit with Leigh Kerfoot and Lizzie Link against the City of Laramie for cutting off the water in Spring Creek.

"We have first rights," they contended, "due to our homestead claims. The City has no authority to divert water from the original course to satisfy the street-side supply into the town."

After much recrimination, the dispute was settled, if not amicably, at least in a workable manner. Even the crustiest remarks made by J.H. Hayford in the columns in his *Daily Sentinel* did not sway the farmers. Water was restored to them, and Hayford was obliged to pull in his horns.

Diana added to the family income by milking cows, selling milk, cream and butter, and selling eggs and poultry from her chicken flock. Due to coyotes and other predators, her chickens had to be kept in a pen. Even then weasels, raccoons and hawks took their toll.

Brother Richard had died in 1875 after having a foot badly crushed in a railroad accident. Mother Bridgit moved in with Diana and the little Browns after Jackson's death. The women worked and the children grew.

According to family legends, Anna became a teacher and went to Hawaii where she met and married a man named Rice. They returned to Wyoming and settled on a ranch southwest of Laramie on Sand Creek. Young Jackson soon joined them and later he moved over the mountains and took up land in the North Platte River valley.

Attractive Josephine fell in love with a cowboy named Skirdin. Family legend has it that Skirdin was Owen Wister's *Virginian*. That may be. If so, he was one of many for Wister always asserted his Virginian was a composite of individuals. He had taken characteristics of numerous men he admired and *created* his hero.

Being in love with a cowboy who seemed destined to make no mark in the world was not Diana's ambition for her attractive daughter. Whether she argued, harangued, or gave "silent treatment" to the subject, Josephine finally bowed to her mother's wishes and gave up the cowboy. She took her broken heart across the mountains and moved in with brother Jackson.

Diana was now alone. She "neighbored," partied and worked diligently at the Catholic Church. Among the frivolous and favorite party games of the time was consulting the table. In doing this, several persons sat at the table, resting their fingertips lightly against the wooden top. With closed eyes they concentrated on summoning the table's spirit. When there came the familiar pulsations from the wood, they were free to ask questions. One tap from the table leg meant NO, two taps meant YES.

One of the group's pleasures was to stir the superstitious young Lizzie Fee. It didn't take much. She refused to sit at the table, instead occupied a rocking chair across the room. Yet she seemed fascinated with the procedures.

"I don't believe in no spirits of the table," she declared, but refused to join the fun. Instead she rocked and watched.

"Spirit, push Lizzie from her chair," the laughing group requested. And Lizzie fell to the floor.

Surprised, angry and humiliated, Lizzie scrambled to her feet and left the house. After much coaxing and promises to respect her person, she was persuaded to return. Still she didn't join the group at the table. She continued to attend the parties and steadfastly remained a spectator whenever they talked to the table.

The year before his death, Jackson K. had "given" a twenty-acre tract to the City of Laramie. It was swamp-ground, and since Spring Creek flowed through the length of Brown's homestead, was considered worthless. Brown received one hundred dollars for the tract. The city tiled and drained it and established a park. For some years it was known as Brown's Park and often thought to have been donated by the attorney M.C. Brown. Later it became the City Park, and finally Undine Park.

It didn't take long for Diana to realize that she was unable to handle the remaining sixty acres of her farm. And the town was growing and stretching eastward and southward in her direction. In 1889, she sold the homestead, reserving one full block for her own use. The lots were quickly taken up and buildings went up. This annexation to the city was called Park View Addition.

∽ A ghost is said to walk in the old Diana Brown house on the corner of Eighth and Steele. (Beery Collection)

Diana then indulged her whim of having a new house. It was built of brick from one of the Laramie yards. It contained eight rooms. It still stands at the corner of Eighth and Steele Street in Laramie; the brick is now covered with a coating of stucco.

Diana indulged her longing for a green space on earth, as much like Ireland as possible. She planted trees, shrubs and masses of flowers. An old barn stood south of her new home, still sheltering her milk cow, her pigs and driving horse.

One tale of those days tells of the city marshal coming to tell Diana of a jail break. He and his men wanted to search her barn for the escapee.

She agreed and walked to the barn with the officers.

"You'd best stay outside, Mrs. Brown," the officer told her. "If he's in there, he may be armed and dangerous."

"Well now," Diana retorted in her fine Irish brogue. "If someone's hid in my barn, I should certainly like to know it."

Apparently no one was found.

Whatever happened to the original log Brown cabin remains a mystery, but there may be an explanation. It concerns a house now standing in South Laramie, moved there from its location at the dead end of Twelfth and Steele streets.

For unnumbered years it had stood on the high-school football field and served as home for various coaches. The core of the house is log, now aged and cured hard as stone. Old cabins didn't always have foundations, only a ground-sill resting either on flat rocks or plain dirt. Moving a cabin was thus a relatively simple procedure.

Robert Burns *in Pioneer Ranches of Wyoming* puzzled over the "disappearance of the Brown cabin." He was fond of Grandma Brown and mourned the loss of the familiar landmark.

There is no real evidence, but this *could* be the explanation: Diana sold her cabin to Carpenter Jacob May who moved it to his lots at Twelfth and Steele and made changes in it for the use of his own family. Many facts hint that it was the Brown cabin.

Diana cordially open her new home to friends and neighbors, and she soon found herself surrounded by them all. She loved the place, and when she died in 1915, seems to have relinquished it with regret. Numerous owners and renters report seeing the specter of "Grandma Brown" in different rooms of the house on Steele Street.

∞

BIBLIOGRAPHICAL ESSAY. Information about Diana and her family has come from many sources. Important information came from the Virginia Toothaker family of Saratoga, Wyoming. Virginia, daughter of Anna Brown Rice, married William Toothaker and lived on the Rice-Brown ranch on the North Platte Valley above Saratoga. It was to this ranch, then owned by Jackson Brown, Jr., that Josephine went after breaking up with her cowboy. Here she met Charles Sanger, a prominent rancher, who helped mend her broken heart. They were married and lived out their years on the famous Sanger ranch near her brother Jackson.

Some of this information was found in the bicentennial edition of the *History of Saratoga* (The Woodlands, Texas: Portfolio Publishing, 1976).

Other information was found in *Pioneer Ranches of Wyoming* by Burns, Gillespie and Richardson, previously cited.

Details of the house Diana built were furnished by John Stenger, one of the owners, and Mrs. Charles Vojé who lived in the house as a young girl. Mae Powell Stone related the incident with the table.

Information on the "Old Wire Road" was furnished by Laureda Anderson of Lebanon, Missouri.

All other information regarding the land and legal transfers may be found in Albany County Records at the Albany County Courthouse in Laramie.

Information on Charles H. Sanger, Josephine Brown Sanger and Anna Brown Rice was obtained from their obituaries.

∽ ∽ ∽ ∽ ∽ ∽ ∽ ∽ ∽ ∽ ∽ ∽ ∽ ∽ ∽

SARSAPARILLA MEAD WAS A POPULAR DRINK ADVERTISED IN THE PIONEER WEST TO QUENCH THIRST, AID DIGESTION AND TO PREVENT FEVER, HEADACHE AND INDIGESTION.

✻

MANY LARAMIE CITY PEOPLE WERE SUPERSTITIOUS ABOUT THANKING A DONOR FOR A GIFT OF A PLANT, LEST THE PLANT DIE.

✻

AMONG THE EARLY SETTLERS OF WELSH DESCENT IT WAS CONSIDERED UNLUCKY TO BUY BEES. TO PREVENT THE BEES FROM DYING THEY WERE BARTERED, NOT BOUGHT. ALSO, THERE WAS A BELIEF THAT BEES SHOULD BE INFORMED OF THE DEATH OF THEIR OWNER. THE NEW OWNER WOULD GO TO THE HIVE AND COMMUNE WITH THE BEES SO HE WOULD BE ACCEPTED BY THEM.

✻

WHITE HORSES ABOUND IN IRISH LEGENDS AND SUPER-STITIONS AND EARLY IRISH SETTLERS IN LARAMIE CITY STILL HELD THE BELIEF. IT WAS THOUGHT THAT A PERSON RIDING ON A WHITE HORSE HAD A GIFT OF GREAT WISDOM AND WAS ESPECIALLY ABLE TO CURE PHYSICAL ILLS.

∽ ∽ ∽ ∽ ∽ ∽ ∽ ∽ ∽ ∽ ∽ ∽ ∽ ∽ ∽

❧ MIST WALKERS

O N CERTAIN MOONLESS nights there is a sinister presence in the alley near the back door of 111 Grand in
Laramie. Steve Brodnovitis, a staff member of the
defunct *Gem City News*, says, "There are unexplainable
things about this town—and this building." The building
stands on the site of the old Tivoli Saloon of Laramie's first
giddy beginnings in 1868.

It carried several different names during its saloon-life, but
the present building, raised in 1893, was first Huempfner's
Rocky Mountain Beer Hall. The building served as saloons, a
cobbler shop, gambling and card rooms, a flower shop, a
rooming house, and even a small factory for hand-made
cigars. More recently it was the site of High Country Books,
then offices of the *Gem City News* with a bed and breakfast on
the upper floor.

Fights, at least one killing and plenty of wife-beatings
took place on the early site.

"That thing back there in the alley is threatening," Steve
said. "I wouldn't think of going out there to investigate.
There's something inside, too. I feel uneasy in the room near
that back door—the same way in the basement.... For me
those places are chilling. No other place in the building gives
me bad vibes."

"I'm not bothered that way," Joan Bassett said. She operates the bed and breakfast on the second floor. "We do have a couple of presences in the hallway and upstairs. I've—We've all heard them—heavy footsteps going up the stairs. There's the smell of tobacco smoke, and lighter footsteps and perfume. There have been movements in our apartment upstairs and in the bed and breakfast area. Nothing threatening, just the knowledge that there is—*some*thing in the building."

Steve likes to walk at night after work. But he says "there's another spot in town where I've felt something special is there. Over at the corner where the Wiseman Jewelry is (Fifth and Ivinson), there is a feeling of utter despair. Such a feeling of desperate loneliness and despair. It's really gripping!"

That could be the spirit of the lovely lady who came to Laramie as a bride. She lived on that corner. Lonely and homesick for her Maryland family and friends, overwhelmed by the raw, open land of wind and grass and no trees, she went insane.

These unquiet spirits, whose highways are usually the night, thrive in Laramie. Sometimes there is only a subtle presence, but often it is a stronger manifestation. Some of Laramie's past residents have even been seen in daylight in different parts of town.

Men lost in the explosion of the railroad shops visit their old homes on the west side. Workmen and their ladies have been heard in happy talk in a house at the corner of Cedar and Sheridan.

"I came onto the porch and heard these voices and laughter," my friend Amelia said. "I thought, uh-oh, someone left the TV on again. As soon as I opened the door all sound was gone. I checked the TV but it was not on. I looked through the whole house; no one was there. There wasn't anything. There just wasn't *any*thing."

"Did it sound like a group? Men and women, or just women?" I asked. "Did you *feel* any presence?"

"No. I felt nothing. I was alone. One time it sounded just like women, talking and laughing. Another time it sounded kind of like a party, men and women. No music, nothing like that. Just talking and laughing. What would you think of that?" Amelia asked with a helpless shrug. "One day my son was in the kitchen. He looked out the window and saw a man sitting on the porch. Just sitting there, like a live person, sitting and resting. He had on a blue work shirt and blue overalls. He was kind of sweaty under his arms and suspenders. He wore a straw hat. He was there only a few minutes, then he disappeared. Just vanished."

The earliest known haunting is at Diana Brown's house at the corner of Eighth and Steele. There, a grandmotherly lady in dust-cap and old fashion clothes has been seen placidly sewing and rocking in a low rocking chair. On occasion the chair has rocked with no phantom in it. This presence is referred to as Grandma Brown, but probably should be called Grandma Herran, Diana Brown's mother.

She hasn't made her presence known to all residents of the house. One of the owners was quite regretful. "...We haven't seen her nor heard a peep in all the time we've lived here. We're quite let down!"

Spirits apparently select when and with whom they want to live, and when to leave. A World War I soldier has appeared three times to a Laramie lady. His appearances were always preceded by a deep chill in the room.

"After that first time I wasn't surprised," my friend told me. "No, I didn't know him. I don't know why he chose to appear to me. He came, just stood there in the corner of the room for a few minutes, then just went. The second time he was all bandaged around the head, and there were other bandages. He sat down. He sat there looking at me—kind of pleading—such sad eyes! He wore the type of uniform World War I soldiers wore—leggin's, that kind of coat. The last time he came, he stood in the same spot as he had the first time. He stood and just looked at me. It was definitely farewell."

Even one of Laramie's soiled doves makes her presence known on occasion. The spirit of Christy Grover, known in her time as "The Blonde" and "Puss Newport," among other aliases, moves on the quiet side—soft rustlings, closing doors, pictures hanging crooked on the walls (which could be caused by passing traffic, for her place, known then as "Grover's Institute" was on Grand Avenue, the main thoroughfare in town.)

Christy's houses of dalliance stood where Madison's Gift Shop and a restaurant, Jacque's of Laramie, now stand. The attractive blond prostitute has been portrayed by Judith Wooderson on occasions of walking tours in Laramie.

"I felt she approved my portrayal," Judy wrote from her present home in Farmington, New Mexico. "I felt she'd had a very sad life.... There is a spot near the alley which seems to 'draw' me."

This could be the location where Christy Grover died of a gunshot wound to the head, a presumed suicide.

Her husband, John Grover, and Monte Arlington, one of Christy's flock, were married some months later, and Monte assumed the position of madam at Grover's Institute. But fear of unknown origin caused Monte to starve herself to death. There is no evidence that her spirit hovers in the vicinity.

At Jacque's where Christy's other house stood, there is "never anything really noticeable, just a feeling that someone is near, watching you," one of the waitresses said. "But of course there is no one."

In another of Laramie's older homes there is a presence which the children enjoy and are proud to call their "own

Luther, a kindly spirit, likes to stand in the upstairs window of this home and look out over the neighborhood. (Beery Collection)

ghost." He's had different names with different families. He's been Garth and Joshua and lately Luther.

Luther manifests himself at his own pleasure. He supervises meal preparations and limits bathroom time for those who read or meditate too long. He appears physically in an upstairs bedroom window on occasion—a figure silhouetted between the drawn window shade and window pane, a space of four to six inches. Neighbors have asked if the "man of the house" was home at those times. Luther likes to stand in the window and look out over "his" street and neighborhood.

He has definite opinions and a temper which he isn't hesitant to express. Yet he has particular regard for "his family" and gives warning of impending changes, or mental suggestions on how to meet a circumstance. The family are pleased to call him friend. Family pets are much aware of Luther's presence, but not fearful.

Not so with another revenant. This angry spirit inhabits another of Laramie's historic homes, the W.H. Holliday house. Before its removal to a rural site, the lovely old building stood at the corner of Garfield and Fourth Streets.

The Holliday family had no spirit-guests while they lived in the house. Nor were there any when the building became a rooming house.

"The Comus Rooms belonged to Ethel Burbank, my sister-in-law," Lydia Zeller stated. "I was there frequently with Ethel and later, when I was manager, there was never any such thing as a ghost. There were no tragic deaths—never a hint of such things. If there is a ghost in that house now, it comes from the move."

She has a point there.

The house now stands on one-time ranch land. The visitant is a cowboy who could have been killed in a range quarrel. Or, the spirit may have been a victim of the gang of hoodlums which ran roughshod over Laramie during its 1868 birth-pangs. The Moore gang lured, or coerced, customers into their deadfall gambling joint at the corner of First and South C [Garfield], got them drunk or doped, then robbed and murdered them without conscience. Some were buried beneath the dirt floor of a back room, but most were hauled out of town and dumped onto the prairie for predators to chew on.

The angry cowboy clumps heavily about the halls of the old Holliday house, scares the cats and dogs, and fidgets with lights and small objects in the house.

"One night our young son got up to go to the bathroom and met this cowboy in the hall. It was *right there, looming* in the dark and coming right at him. It was a very traumatic experience," Sheryl Woolfe said. "Someone started the story that he rattles pans in the kitchen, but that isn't so. It's his tramping about that's bothersome. We try to ignore it."

There are two Georges who have manifested themselves in town. One is a resident of the J.T. Holliday house, now Meyer's Apartments, at 719 Grand.

∞ *The angry cowboy who lives in the historic W.H. Holliday home scares the cats and dogs. (*Beery Collection)

"We call him George, for no particular reason," Mrs. Meyers writes. "My daughter has seen him, but I haven't. I have felt his presence at times, though, especially in the attic. Others have heard him. Things disappear, then reappear in odd places… the usual tricks, I guess."

The family cat, a dignified, serene creature, would arch her back, fluff her tail and hiss at "nothing." She never ran, however. She may have had an equal-spooking-term agreement with George.

Years ago two roomers at the house quarreled over a young teen-age girl and one was seriously wounded when the squabble erupted into gunplay. The battle occurred near the soda beds west of town, however, not at the house.

The other George haunted across town.

"He was with us for years," Betty related. "We were used to him. He'd fiddle with the lights, or the telephone, move things about and so on. But then our little granddaughter became troubled, didn't want to be in a certain room. She'd fuss and cry for no apparent reason and that sort of thing bothered all of us and couldn't be tolerated, so we exorcised George."

"How did you accomplish that?"

"We joined hands and said 'In the name of Jesus, GO!' We haven't been troubled with George since!"

∞

BIBLIOGRAPHICAL ESSAY. Interviews with people in Laramie have provided material for this interesting tale. Most of the people interviewed asked not to be identified, because they didn't want anyone to think them "peculiar." I have used the first name of some of them. The Carol Barnes family do not mind being named. Luther lives with them. I believe in Luther. I have felt his presence at times when writing about him, and have had it impressed upon me by him that I've written enough articles (three) concerning him, and he wants to rest. He is a kindly soul, and I hope he does not object to this additional mention.

There are other visitants in Laramie, and hints of some, but informants asked not to be quoted in a book and wanted their stories to remain unprinted.

Many people scoff at the idea of ghosts, yet there is much that is unexplainable about such manifestations—more than the *coincidence* that is often attributed to unusual happenings. Sometimes these occurrences are labeled "evil." How, then, can it be explained when the "unexplainable" definitely saves a life, or prevents some tragedy? True, some may be "evil," but there are also the good and beneficial. I believe in the beneficial and good.

✣ Gypsy's Warning

THE GYPSY'S WARNING
"Trust him not, O Gentle maiden
Though his voice is low and sweet
Heed him not, who kneels before you,
Softly pleading at your feet.
Though thy life is in its morning
Trust not this, thy happy lot;
Listen to the Gypsy's Warning
And gentle lady, trust him not."

IT WAS CHRISTMAS EVE 1868, and Harriet Adelia Rice was singing the "Gypsy's Warning" at the great celebration in the Railroad Hotel in Laramie City.

As her sweet young voice sent the words of warning to all the young women in the party room, Harriet paid the lyrics little heed herself. Her eyes searched the crowd for the handsome face of Henry H. Richards.

Richards, a grocer, and a "refined" man from the East, was considered one of the highly eligible bachelors of the frontier town. Certainly he was handsome, well-educated, reliable and ambitious. And he returned Harriet's interest.

Harriet's father, Samuel "Pap" Rice, was a freighter and due to his work, seldom home, so her mother was the main factor in the life of the teenage girl. Euphemia Rice, or Emia as she was called, owned and operated the famous Tivoli saloon and was owner of a number of prime lots in the business section of Laramie City.

Harriet helped her mother in the Tivoli. It was a place of comparative quiet so far as decorum went on the frontier.

Emia, Harriet and H.H. were a part of that riotous evening in October 1868, when three toughs were hung and many of the others run out of town. The plans had been made in a back room of the Tivoli.

Harriet and H.H. Richards became well acquainted during their first years in Laramie, so it was not surprising when they decided to go into business together.

H.H. turned over operation of his grocery business to his brother Charles, and he and Harriet opened a restaurant on a lot owned by Harriet's mother across the street from the Tivoli. They called their place K-2-Tor.

Even the mysterious name was no help, there was too much competition and "by mutual consent" their contract was dissolved at the end of the first month.

H.H. and his brother Charles became partners in the brick-making business. Again the Rice property came in handy. The brothers set up their yard on Pap's ranch where his freight outfits were kept. They located the brick business just south of town where travelers and emigrant wagons crossed the Big Laramie River, and where one of the slaughterhouses stood, so blood and animal hair were handy to use in their brick making.

Harriet returned to work in the Tivoli while the brothers operated the grocery store and brickyard. The brickyard went broke. Charlie went to California. Henry had to close the grocery store and look for a job. He found one as a clerk in the John Wanless drygoods store.

On March 9, 1870, he and Harriet Adelia Rice were married. The handsome, refined Richards and his attractive wife built a snug little brick house "way out" on the east edge of town. The site is now in mid-city at 517 South Seventh Street.

Their marriage was harmonious. Both were busy, she at home, he in the Wanless store and in all the civic activities he favored.

Richards was successively Clerk of the Court, Albany County Commissioner, twice Assistant Secretary of the Third Legislature at Cheyenne, and was appointed Clerk of the House of the state legislature. At home, he helped organize the Presbyterian Church and served as a member of its Board of Trustees. He was one of the early advocates for the Literary Association in Laramie and contributed much to the town library. He later ran for Probate Judge "with no blemish on his name or record." Perhaps he was too perfect. He lost.

Then Harriet became ill. The specific problem was not identified, but the *Laramie Sentinel* spent much time in commiserating with H.H. Richards.

Her recovery was long and slow. Their marriage suffered.

They were sued by Mast and Goodwin for money due for building their little brick house, a sum less than fifty dollars but almost a fortune in those times when *high* wages were twenty-five dollars a month.

Wanless sold his store and went to Colorado. Henry found work in the old Blue Front. The Trabings had converted their one-time saloon and vaudeville house to a wholesale-retail grocery and outfitting store. Richards became their chief clerk and manager.

Harriet's health was still delicate and so was their marriage. H.H. moved out and took a room downtown. She, with no source of income, and no support from her refined husband, lost their little house for non-payment of taxes.

On January 4, 1879, Harriet filed for divorce stating: "...on or about January 1st, 1878, the said Henry H. Richards, regardless of his marriage covenants and duties willfully deserted your complainant without just and reasonable cause...." The decree was granted April 5, and Harriet went to Colorado's North Park area where her parents operated a stage stop just south of Pinkhampton.

H.H. took a job as Census Enumerator for the year 1880 and upon his return to Laramie learned that his once loved Harriet had become Mrs. Howard Peasley of what is now Walden, Colorado.

Harriet hadn't learned from the Gypsy's Warning. Her second husband was another refined, well-educated man from the East.

Henry immediately went to North Park, to Teller with its promising mine-fields. He soon moved a few miles north of Teller to Sage Hen Draw (or Creek) and established a store. He was also appointed postmaster at the new post office there. This became the second site for the town of Walden.

Richards was highly regarded in North Park and was soon given the nickname "Granny," whether because of his temperate habits or the fact that he still acted as a gentleman in that rough-and-tumble community.

He operated his store in the same building with the post office and bought supplies from his former bosses, the Trabing Brothers of Laramie.

As always happened, it was necessary for the store to extend credit, and some people left the Park without paying. Others were slow in settling their bills, still others were held up due to low prices paid for their livestock or hay. This put Richards behind in paying the Trabings, and they sued. Twice. The second time they attached "one team of horses and harness and one Cooper wagon." So Henry was left with no way to travel or haul supplies from Trabing's warehouse in Teller.

Then Harriet Peasley was appointed postmistress of Walden in 1889, and again in 1991, the second time as Mrs. Henry Docker.

Since post office and store occupied the same building it stirs curiosity about the daily contact between Richards and his one-time love.

All trace of H.H. "Granny" Richards is lost after 1895.

Harriet apparently lived in North Park the rest of her life. Perhaps her two marriage ventures with cultured gentlemen reminded her of the Gypsy's Warning. Her third marriage, to Henry Docker, a freighter, put her in a more familiar, and possibly happier, atmosphere.

∞

BIBLIOGRAPHICAL ESSAY. The House built for H.H. Richards and Harriet Adelia Rice Richards is the house of the Dalton legend (see *The Dalton Gang* in this book). Records concerning this ownership were county records and news items of the period.

Information on persons in the North Park-Walden area is taken from the book "North Park" with permission from the author Hazel Gresham (Steamboat Springs, Colorado: *Steamboat Pilot*, 1975).

∞ *Billy Bacon ran a saloon at Fort Fetterman across the river from the One-Mile Ranch, which was often called the Hog Ranch. Bacon lost his leg when he met a bull team on a bridge and refused to back up. (Pioneer Museum, Douglas, Wyoming)*

❦ BLACK DAY AT THE HOG RANCH

THE COUNTRY WAS filling up. Freighters' wagons were more numerous than emigrant wagons. Indians, beaten, brutalized and shunted onto the most uninviting reservations, remained proud and unconquered, but were no longer the menace they once had been.

Ranchers, squatters and cattlemen moved in. The "Virginians" and the "Trampases" had not yet arrived, but cowboys and cattle pocked the short-grass country of Wyoming.

In 1883, the largest livestock round-up of the Platte River Valley occurred. Old Fort Fetterman became the central meeting place for one hundred and fifty or more cowboys.

The military fort [near what is now Douglas] had been abandoned in 1882 and Fetterman, no longer a government facility, became one of the wildest cattle towns on the frontier.

Some of the cowboys gave up the range and adopted a higher-paying, but more dangerous, style of living. John D. Lawrence and Jack Sanders did that. They became partners in operating the One-Mile Ranch, a saloon and bawdy house across the North Platte River from Fetterman.

Lawrence, cowboy and ex-ranch cook, was a high-tempered Irishman with an itchy trigger finger. Jack Sanders appeared in the Fort Laramie-Fetterman area about 1882. He was known as a tough one—a loud-mouth, gambler and gunslinger. The pair seemed to hit it off in fine shape.

Their dive, legally called the One-Mile Ranch, was less delicately known as the Hog Ranch, although it never saw a hog. So notorious was it that it is still shown on Wyoming maps as a historic site.

Across the river in one of the buildings remaining on the old fort grounds, Billy Bacon ran the saloon he bought after being forced to quit bronc busting. Bacon's mulish disposition had cost him half a leg and his career as a bronco buster when he met a bull team pulling a loaded freight wagon on a narrow bridge spanning a mountain stream.

There was no passing room. The two men exchanged loud and heated remarks. The bullwhacker could not back his oxen and wagon, and Bacon would not retreat.

Bacon's horse began to buck. He was thrown off and fell beneath the bulls' feet. They panicked and trampled the man and his horse. The heavy wagon ran over Bacon's leg, crushing it. The horse was killed.

Bacon's right leg had to be amputated below the knee, ending his bronc riding. He probably was fitted with one of the newfangled cork legs. It didn't improve his disposition.

He tried ranching for a few years, then bought the saloon in Fetterman. He and Sanders and Lawrence were competitors and friends.

In 1884, the fall round-up was again in the Fetterman vicinity. Visitors to the saloons engaged in their regular boozing, brawling and bragging. Most of the talk was just a pastime, but sometimes a brag was pushed to a serious turn. This may have been true of two of W. P. Rickett's riders, John Fenix and Frank Wallace. Their swaggering about and tough talk in Bacon's saloon centered on the Hog Ranch and its owners.

"We'll just go over there and show those guys how to run that place," John Fenix bragged over his cups.

"If you're smart you'll stay away from there," Ricketts told them. "I know John Lawrence. He is a nervous Irishman. He used to work for me and I know. Stay away or he'll kill you."

"Aw, he ain't so much," Fenix scoffed, apparently taking the boss's words as a dare, and he and Wallace took off across the river.

About three hours later a fast-riding cowboy clattered into Fetterman and told Ricketts, "You sure can't fool with that John Lawrence! He killed one of those fellows and shot an eye out for the other one!"

The coroner's inquest brought out that the pair had accosted Lawrence in the Hog Ranch saloon. Wallace had taunted Lawrence, asking why he "looked scared to death." Lawrence had replied, "I ain't so scared."

Fenix then said he had heard that "someone told Lawrence he had made threats to come over and run this place."

"Yes, I heard that," Lawrence told him.

Fenix snapped, "It's a lie. Who told you?"

Quietly Lawrence replied, "That's not important. What is important is I've paid my money for this place and I intend to run it myself."

More words followed. Fenix pulled his pistol and shot, hitting Lawrence in the shoulder.

"I tried to grab his pistol," Lawrence testified at the hearing, "and got my left hand powder burnt. He shot at me again as I was going out the door. And I shot at him. He yelled, 'Frank, kill the last son of a bitch of them!' I don't know if I hit him or not. I turned around as soon as I got out of doors and saw Frank Wallace standing behind the entrance door. He shot at me and I shot back. Then he shot two or three more times. John Fenix jumped out the door and shot deliberately at John [Jack] Sanders. I jumped back into the house and got my shotgun from behind the bar. I came outside and Frank

Wallace was standing at the horse rack with his gun resting on it. He took dead aim at me and shot. I shot back. He fell behind the hitch rack and the horses. When I went to him he didn't speak or move. I went back into the house. While I was inside Wallace got up, got on his horse and rode off. John Sanders and I got on our horses and rode over to Fetterman. I didn't know Fenix was shot until we got to Fetterman."

Lawrence got the slug taken out of his shoulder. A wild shot had hit one of the Hog Ranch floozies in the neck and shoulder. Her name was reported to be Ella Watson although it may have been Ella Wilcox or Ella Wilson. Some believe she was the same Ella Watson who later was known as Cattle Kate and was lynched as a cattle rustler.

The coroner's jury returned a verdict of self-defense and exonerated both Lawrence and Sanders.

Frank Wallace, who had saved his hide by playing possum, ever afterward wore a patch over his dead eye and became known as Pretty Frank. "The homeliest man I ever set eyes on," one woman said.

Lawrence and Sanders chipped in for Fenix's funeral and to make up a purse for his young teenaged brother who elected to remain with Rickett's riders.

Not long afterward Sanders was involved in another scrape. Thomas Diamond, a muleskinner, and another freighter got into a squabble. Diamond pulled a knife and went after the other man. Sanders objected and Diamond turned on him with the knife. Sanders snatched a shotgun from the freight wagon and fired. Diamond fell dead.

Dr. J.H. Bradley reported to the coroner's jury that Diamond died "of eight holes in the breast and three in the left shoulder...." The jury said Sanders acted in self-defense.

It seemed to be the general opinion of the community. Live rough. Die rough.

In May 1885, a coroner's jury was impanelled to decide the cause of death of an unknown man near Sage Creek Stage Ranch eighteen miles north of Fetterman. The cork-legged Billy Bacon and Jack Sanders were subpoenaed and drove together in a buggy to the site.

The jury found the deceased had "died of a gunshot wound which had entered his head from behind and came out out his right eye, leaving powder marks on hair, shirt, coat and hat. The wound was inflicted by party or parties unknown to the jury."

They were of the further opinion that the unknown man "did not inflict the wound himself."

The signatures of William L. Bacon and John Sanders, appearing with the other jurors' were both written in bold legible script. The handwriting could be construed to represent the overweening confidence and egotism of the two men.

An interesting sidelight is that Sanders does not spell his name with a "u" although it appears as "Saunders" now in many tales of the man.

One of the stories about Sanders tells of a call he made on Dr. Amos Barber, operator of the Fetterman Hospital.

"I understand you clean teeth," Sanders drawled. "I want a job done."

Barber explained that he was a medical doctor, not a dentist. He recommended a tooth powder to the caller.

The gambler drew his gun and informed the doctor he wanted his teeth cleaned now. He got the job done with Barber's own toothbrush. Barber charged him five dollars and threw in the toothbrush. Both men apparently were satisfied with the deal.

Life in Fetterman and at the Hog Ranch continued as usual—boozing, brawling, bragging and fornicating.

Mary Potter, of the Hog Ranch, killed herself with an overdose of laudanum. A man named Clark "came to his death

falling from the top of a mess wagon fracturing his skull."
Another cowboy, lovesick for one of the Hog Ranch girls,
looked into a mirror and watched himself commit suicide. He
left a note for his lady love. Jack Sanders was a member of
most of the coroner's juries that looked into these occurrences.

On September 16, 1885, an "Agreement to enter into partnership to conduct retail liquor business and stock business as
equal partners" was filed at the office of the Albany County
Clerk in Laramie. [There were still only five counties in
Wyoming at that time. Fetterman was in Albany County.]

The agreement listed "19 head horses and mules and 8 milk
cows. Furniture and Faro layout, two fiddles at the place
known as One-Mile Ranch, and Bacon's building used formerly as hospital and saloon building, all out-buildings, cooking utensils, bar fixtures belonging to both places, and liquor
and provisions on hand." The instrument was signed by Martha
J. Sanders and Mrs. Frances Bacon at Fetterman, Wyoming.

Martha J. was evidently Mrs. John Sander's legal name,
she also used the name "Viola." Frances Bacon is listed on the
1880 census as "Rebecca." Billy Bacon frequently referred to
her as "Mrs. Sow Belly."

It is possible the partnership of Sanders and Bacon was
really a partnership of the wives, although it was publicly
accepted as being between the men. Taxes on "Fetterman
property with improvements" were charged to John Sanders.

How the business progressed is uncertain. Mrs. Sanders
informed the men that the business needed more girls from
Cheyenne and the men should see to it, instead of drinking up
all the liquor and arguing.

On December 9, 1885, the two men were going over books
at the Bacon saloon in town, and according to witnesses, were
having disagreements. They separated and later met at the Hog
Ranch for more book work. When they finished that stint they

came out into the barroom and their disagreements still rode them heavily.

Bacon left, only to return a short time later and truculently accost Sanders. Court testimony provides their conversation.

"I hear you're saying you can down me."

"No. I never said so," Sanders replied.

"I think you did, for I've been told so."

"Well, whoever told you that is a damned liar."

"Mr. Bacon, Jack never said any such thing," Mrs. Sanders interposed and rested her hand on his arm.

"I wouldn't take your word under oath," Bacon snapped at her, shaking off her hand.

Sanders said, "Hold on now, let's not go too fast here. Whoever told you I said that is a liar."

Bacon stepped over where Jack sat and slapped him in the face. "If you think you can get the drop on me, now's the time to try." And he stepped back, right hand poised.

Mrs. Sanders jumped between the two men and reached for Bacon's pistol. Bacon shoved her aside and drew his gun from the waistband of his trousers. He shot at Sanders. There was a general scramble of people to get out of range or out of the building. The noise of gunfire filled the room.

J.D. Lawrence told the coroners jury, "I saw Mr. Sanders jump toward the bar. Bacon fired again. Sanders snapped his pistol at Bacon, snapped again, and then the pistol went off. Sanders was retreating and Bacon following. The next shot was fired by Bacon as he got near the door. Bacon went outside and met Louis Burr and told him, 'I'm shot. Take me home.'

"Mr. Sanders got up and started to follow Bacon but Mrs. Sanders pulled him back inside. Sanders then went and got a shotgun and came downtown bareheaded. He went down in front of his and Bacon's saloon and called for Blondy. John Ryan came to the door and Sanders asked where Bacon was.

Ryan said he was upstairs in bed, shot. Jack kind of staggered off the sidewalk and said 'Someone take me home. I'm shot.'"

Lawrence stated he had disarmed Sanders and took him home. He helped the gambler undress and put him to bed.

"He was wounded in the abdomen above the waistband of trousers. He said Bacon shot him. Sanders reached for his pistol after Bacon fired the first shot. I could see Bacon all the time but could not see Sanders all the time after the second shot by Bacon. There were present Neal Connors, John Worth, T.E. Toliver and two women besides Mrs. Sanders."

Connors's story agreed with that of Lawrence, except he said he didn't know who fired the first shot for he had left at the first signs of trouble.

John Worth stated the first shot was fired by Bacon after he had slapped Sanders. Sanders drew his pistol after Bacon's first shot. Four shots were fired. Three were Bacon's. Sanders got off one shot, but his pistol snapped on three additional cartridges which did not fire.

James Sanders, Jack's brother, was in Fetterman and when he heard the shooting he "went over to Bacon and Sanders's Bar and opened the door and told them there was shooting over at the Hog Ranch. They all rushed out the door, and one of the fellows made the remark, 'Reed told a pack of lies on Sanders and Bacon.'"

James Sanders testified further that Jack came to him and shook hands and said, "Goodbye. I'm shot by Bacon." James squared his shoulders, but his voice shook as he continued his testimony. "Jack told me it was a put-up job and he didn't think he could live. He told me 'they' had taken the cartridges out of his pistol and put others in. He said he always carried five new ones with one chamber empty."

Sanders died that afternoon.

The coroner's jury found that Jack Sanders came to his

death by means of a gunshot wound fired by a pistol in the hands of William Bacon. And they requested the detention of said William Bacon.

Bacon wasn't going anywhere anyway. He had been hit by a shot that Sanders had fired from the floor. The bullet angled upward and lodged in Bacon's throat.

A doctor, summoned by telegraph from Fort McKinney, tried to retrieve the bullet from Bacon's throat. It slipped down into the man's windpipe and choked him to death, so it was a turnabout type of killing.

Sanders had told his brother James, "I wouldn't have got shot but somebody tampered with my gun."

Who?

∞

BIBLIOGRAPHICAL ESSAY. As usual, the *Laramie Sentinel* provided the first hint of the doin's at the Hog Ranch. Albany County Records; Stanley Lass, caretaker at the old Fort Fetterman site; and copies of articles in *Douglas* (Wyoming) *Budget* and *Casper Tribune-Herald* (1948) provided additional information.

Copies of coroner's inquests into shooting scrapes at the Hog Ranch were obtained from the State Museum.

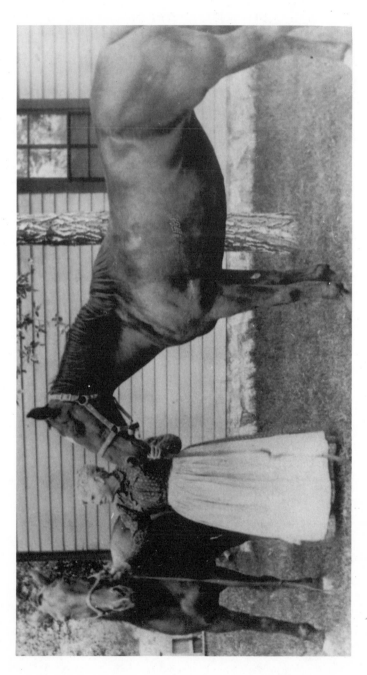

Aunt Fronie loved horses and her skill in handling them was respected by even the most discriminating horseman. (Beery Collection)

✤ Meet Aunt Fronie

HER NAME WAS Sophronia Hutchinson Towle. To her family and friends she was "Fronie." To a pair of neighbor boys she was "Auntie Towle," a kind lady who seemed to like them, but who they "sure didn't want to cross." She gave one of them a Teddy bear—one of his first toys.

Fronie's family, the Hutchinsons, migrated from Maine to Wisconsin, then Minnesota, and finally to Iowa. They raised horses.

Part of the Hutchinson family formed a singing group and entertained Civil War Soldiers—an early-day U.S.O. known as "The Singing Yankees."

Fronie didn't sing. She liked horses and from early girlhood developed marvelous skill in handling them. Her horsemanship was highly praised. She wore the popular divided skirt and rode equally well astride or side-saddle, or even bareback.

Fronie was twenty-seven, an "old maid," when she and William Towle were married. Towle was a native of Maine, too, and related to the P.J. Towle who developed the famous maple-flavored "Log Cabin Syrup."

Will and Fronie came to Laramie City in 1874 and built a little frame house just beyond the north city limit. They set out a row of sweet French lilacs on their north lot line. They may have felt the lilacs would make up for the lack of trees on the grass-blown plains. Or maybe they just loved lilacs.

They soon sold that property and for five hundred dollars bought a relinquishment to a 160-acre homestead on the Little Laramie River and became ranchers. They named their new home Meadow Lawn Ranch. Isaac Bird, the previous owner, had put up only a one-room log shack and a small barn. The Towles added their own improvements: a decent log house, good tight barns, sheds and pole corrals. They raised horses and cattle, but mostly horses.

The years Will and Fronie lived and worked on the Little Laramie were hard ones. Fronie worked right along with Will—digging post holes, stringing fence, building pole corrals and pens, and putting up a barn, which is as tight and solid today as when it was raised. Fronie wielded hammer, axe, saw, and hatchet as well as did her husband. It was said Will worked himself to death on the ranch where "...he had acquired a competence...."

Will suffered grievous injury in a ranch accident and spent his last years crippled and paralyzed. Fronie spent those years running the ranch, working the horses, and caring for her invalid husband. Nothing is written of the energies Fronie expended.

After Will's death in 1893, Fronie's sister, Aurelia, and husband, Jonas H. (Jake) Farr, came to help her with the ranch. Fronie owned the ranch, but it soon became known as "Farr's." Farr tended the cattle and was the "bossman."

The principal work on the ranch was raising and breaking horses, and this was Fronie's element.

"Everybody remembers those horses," one old-timer exclaimed. "And to own a Towle horse was to own a prize."

Englishman Robert Homer, of the well-known Flag Ranch, went to buy a pair of Fronie's horses. He had settled on a black and a gray, and cowboy Charley Frazier rode into the corral to rope the horses. The strange horse and rider and his whirring lasso startled the animals. They began to cut up and mill about.

Fronie sharply told the rider to leave them alone, and picking up a pair of halters, walked into the corral, called the horses to her and put the halters on them. It was this team that Homer often drove, hitched to his famous yellow-wheeled buggy.

In 1901, Sophronia turned the operation of her ranch over to her sister and brother-in-law, and bought back the little house she and Will had built in town.

The house was now well within the city environs, but there were no ordinances against having animals on the premises. Fronie brought four of her favorite horses to town. She hitched her pair of white driving horses to her red buggy and drove on her various errands about town. She also brought a fine gray she called Gypsy and one she called Clyde. She allowed them to graze on her verdant lawn, careful to keep them from the masses of flowers she raised every summer.

Bill Mathison, the neighbor boy who received the Teddy bear, related "Auntie Towle sometimes drove a one-horse buggy with Gyp. Sometimes she drove a two-horse buckboard, and sometimes she took me and my brother along when she drove to the store, so we could get stuff for our mother. She took me and my brother out to the fair once. The fairgrounds was out between what is now Eighteenth and Twenty-fifth streets. Besides her other qualities, Auntie Towle was really careful with money. She drove out to the fairgrounds, then stopped and told my brother and me to get in back under the tarp. We did, because we never wanted to cross her. She took us in to the fairgrounds—and saved herself the ten cent admission for each of us.

"Auntie Towle was a kind woman, but pretty rough spoken. The Towles had brought out that batch of sweet lilacs when they moved from Iowa, and the bushes flourished and made a dandy hedge, with an opening through which Auntie Towle came every day to visit us. Mother enjoyed back-door neighbors, as did everyone those days, but the daily calls were often disruptive. She told Dad they needed a fence. Dad was stringing fence when over Auntie came and asked what he was doing."

"'I'm putting up a fence,' he told her.

"'Well, put a gate in here,' she said.

"'There's not going to be a gate,' Dad replied.

"'Well, I want a gate. Put a gate in here,' she ordered. He put in the gate, right where she wanted it.

"She always had masses of flowers to cut and give bouquets to shut-ins and take out to the cemetery. She'd put them in buckets or cans of water and drive either Gypsy hitched to the one-horse rig or the white team and red-wheeled buggy."

In 1911, Sophronia sold her ranch and her beloved horses, but she kept Clyde and Gypsy. No record has been found as to the fate of Clyde, but Gypsy was alive in 1919.

During the terrible epidemic of Spanish influenza in 1918-1919, Fronie died of bronchial pneumonia. Her hand-written will requested that her horse Gypsy be chloroformed. He was old, and it was done.

Frank and Jean Croonberg now own the ranch which was once the "competence" of William Towle. There is considerable praise written for the work of Will and for the Towle horses. There is very little mention of Sophronia Towle and her efforts and years of untiring toil on their ranch.

∞

BIBLIOGRAPHICAL ESSAY. Many sources furnished Aunt Fronie's story, including the county records at Albany County Courthouse and the 1885 map of Laramie City.

I am indebted to Irene Prahl, William Mathison, Leslie Crawford, and Agnes Wright Spring for personal recollections of Mrs. Towle.

Frank Croonberg, who now lives on the Towle Ranch, also added to her history by sharing his correspondence with members of the Hutchinson family of Wisconsin.

As in many of these chapters, *Pioneer Ranches of Albany County* provided information.

The Laramie newspapers furnished little information about Sophronia Towle. Since she was such a forthright, spirited lady it may be expected that Editor Hayford would withhold praise for her accomplishments as a ranchwoman. He did comment on her horsemanship. She may have ruffled his feathers by doing a man's work while caring for her paralyzed husband.

Nevertheless many remember her with praise.

∞ *Bronco Sam Stewart was known as a fine rider and a good hand with cattle. Jealousy over his attractive wife led to a shoot-out and his death.* (Courtesy Agnes Burns)

❦ Bronco Sam

Samuel L. Willis, in his autobiography *Life Of An Old Cowboy,* tells how he and a friend went from Northern Colorado in the winter of 1873 "up to the E. W. Whitcomb ranch on the Box Elder (Dakota Territory) to take some lessons at bronc riding from a black man known as Bronco Sam, who was the best rider I ever saw, and I've seen quite a few...."

Sam Stewart (Bronco Sam) was one of the best durn cowboys that ever choused a cow and one of the best bronc riders that ever rode on the Laramie Plains—or any other place.

Bill Nye, early day newspaper man and founder of Laramie's famous *Boomerang,* said Sam was "...not a white man, an Indian, a Greaser or a Negro, but he had the nose of an Indian warrior, the curly hair of an African and the courtesy and equestrian grace of a Spaniard."

Sam was all of that. His father was of African descent, his mother Indian and Spanish. He was born in 1852 in south Texas and spoke fluent, beautiful Castilian Spanish. He appeared to have some schooling, yet he couldn't write.

Sam was Samuel Stewart or Stuart or Steward, but that didn't matter. He always signed his name the same way—with a big "x."

Sam grew up around horses and loved and understood them it seemed. It was his ambition to become a top horse handler. As soon as he was old enough, he signed on with a cow outfit and became cook's helper, chuckwagon driver and late night herder. He soon graduated to wrangler.

He trailed north with the cattle herds and in 1872 was in the North Platte Valley around Fort Laramie and Laramie Peak. By the Spring of '74, he was over on the rolling grasslands of the Laramie Plains working for Tom Alsop.

Sam was a handy person, always around in an emergency. He was on hand when young Johnny Alsop fell into a raging flood on the Big Laramie River.

The three-year-old child was hard to find in the muddy, boiling current, but Sam made a lucky grab and caught the little boy's dress tail. Willing hands hauled the boy and man from the raging snow-water torrent and praises were heaped upon the modest cowboy by all the crew and the grateful Alsops. He even received a new felt hat to replace the one carried away in the flood.

When Sam was in Laramie City, he hung out at the Frontier Hotel at the corner of Second and South C [Garfield] Streets—or across the street at the big livery barn.

He was standing in the barn doorway during one of the severe electric storms usual to the valley. A lightning bolt struck the barn, setting fire to the building and hay, killing a horse in the corral and stunning Sam Stewart and another man. They recovered, but Sam lost his new prized overcoat in the blaze.

Sam was in town on the hot summer day when a team broke loose from where it was tied and raced down the street smarting from horsefly stings. Chickens, pigs and kids scattered in all directions while a bevy of dogs raced hysterically with the horses.

Sam dashed into the street, caught the cheekstrap of one bridle and brought the team to a halt. His shoulder was wrenched in the process and a leg bruised by the horse, but he saved the wagon with its load of groceries.

And when Leigh Kerfoot's eight-year-old son was lost on the featureless grassy Laramie Plains, it was Sam who found the body the next spring.

When four of Alsop's cowboys found a mountain lion trapped in a deep rock pit in the Chimney Rock cluster near the Colorado line, Sam roped the cat and hauled him out. They shot the frightened, fighting predator which measured eight feet from nose to tail and brought him to town for everyone to see.

When anyone wanted a bronco tamed it was Sam Stewart they called, for he "had the touch" and could gentle down the wildest.

Sam was a straight-up rider. He never used a quirt on his mount or pulled leather. If he saw any rider pulling leather "he'd ride alongside and whip the offending hand on the horn with his quirt until the rider let loose and rode as he should."

A newspaper item related that "Black Sam" and Tom Alsop were arrested for stealing some cattle from Edward Ivinson's herd. The trial jury freed the two and the newspaper gleefully reported that "Evergreen" Ivinson had to pay all costs. The public understood that Sam was no thief.

In January 1877, Sam got the job as mail carrier from Laramie City to Fort Laramie, a distance of one hundred miles or better. He made the trip once a week.

February found him in an encounter with Cheyenne Indians. The *Laramie Daily Sentinel* reported that: "Sam Stewart, better known as Bronco Sam, our indomitable Fort Laramie mail carrier, came in last evening having run the gauntlet of Indians from Jack Dalton's to the top of the hills east of here. Sam got to Dalton's night before last and stayed overnight. That day Dalton and his men had been having a fight with 25 to 30 Indians.

"The Indians were afoot except for six horses. Dalton's party had killed one Indian and captured four of their six horses. They sent to Fort Russell for help and 25 soldiers got out to the ranch yesterday. They, in company with Dalton and his men, started after the Indians.

"Being mounted they had a good show of overtaking them, but Sam says if they had the soldiers would have been licked.

"...Sam came part way with the soldiers and chanced the rest alone. The Indians were evidently on a horse stealing expedition and stockmen of this valley had better be on the lookout...."

There were other reports of Indians "depredating" between Fort Laramie and Laramie City and other reports of close calls, escapes and fatal encounters. But not for Sam. He made his weekly ride in safety until he was caught in a sudden heavy blizzard the spring of 1882.

The wild storm raged for four days and no word was heard from Bronco Sam; he was given up for lost. The town mourned for the popular black rider.

But Sam was a sturdy one, and on March 3, 1882, the *Laramie Daily Sentinel* carried the banner headline: "BRONCO SAM SAFE!" The sorrow turned to rejoicing.

Sam had a good reason for surviving that vicious spring storm, and it appeared in the *Sentinel* on April 3, 1882.

"We chronicle this week the marriage of Sam Stewart, widely known as Bronco Sam. Sam is one of the old landmarks of the border and deservedly popular with everybody. His bride is a full-blooded Indian and a good looking lass, too."

Her name was Kitty.

The *Sentinel* praised his skill in handling horses. Sam was good at taming hot-blooded horses all right, but marriage proved a different matter. On September 9, five months after their wedding, Sam shot Kitty.

Kitty was visiting their next-door neighbor who took in washing. The laundress was mending underwear for one of her bachelor customers while he waited for his bundle of laundry.

The laundress said: "You'd better buy yourself some new underwear, mister. I can't mend these again—nothing here!"

The three laughed. Bronco Sam entered the room just as Kitty was saying: "You should see my husband's—he's wearing nothing but darnings!"

And Sam said, "Well, my dear, you won't have to darn them anymore" and shot her.

John Alsop, whose life Sam had saved from the flooded Big Laramie, wrote to a friend in 1951, "Sam shot his wife and the man with her, then shot himself through the breast. He wouldn't tell his friends about it."

"Then Bronco Sam left the house, walked back across the square and collapsed in a pool of blood." Friends carried him to a doctor.

At the time of the incident the newspaper did not mention the bachelor customer being shot, only that the town "was well acquainted with the occurrence," and "Sam shot in a fit of jealousy."

Gossip linked Kitty and the bachelor in an intimate relationship. However evidence given to the coroner's jury by the laundress and the bachelor customer in no way supported the gossip.

Kitty died three days later. The "good-looking full-blooded Indian lass" of the *Sentinel's* wedding announcement became a "half-breed squaw" in the tale of the tragedy.

Sam lived for ten days.

The newspaper expressed the shock and sorrow of the community and added its own high accolade: "Sam was popular with everyone. He did not drink to excess."

"Why did you shoot yourself, Sam? You didn't have to. We would see that you got off," Alsop wrote that he had told Sam.

Probably.

But that wouldn't have healed Sam's broken heart or washed away the remorse he felt for believing gossip about his beloved Kitty.

∞

BIBLIOGRAPHICAL ESSAY. The *Laramie Sentinel* frequently and admiringly mentioned this sensational bronc rider.

Pioneer Ranches of Wyoming gives a fairly detailed story of Sam, his procedure for taming broncos, and quotes from a letter written to Dr. Burns by John Alsop, who was pulled from the flooded Laramie River by Sam.

Court records of the inquests after Kitty and Sam died present a different picture than the public one.

It appears that Sam's jealousy was aroused by "friends" reporting or implying that Kitty was unfaithful. Since Sam's work took him from home for days at a time, these remarks (whether made seriously or in jest) found fertile ground.

The inquest showed that the shooting was needless.

❧ Martha and Mary

Martha: Petticoat Shylock

"M RS. STICKNEY WAS a small woman, very attractive and quite prim and correct," Lucille Glenn remi nisced. "She never left her house without her hat and gloves, and you knew very well she kept all the social rules of the day. She had beautiful white hair which her hats set off in fine style. I remember her clothes were so nice, especially one suit of horse-hair fabric."

"Horse hair? In a fabric?"

"Yes. Somehow the horse hair was woven into a fine fabric—maybe like sheep's hair (or wool). Her suit was black with white points of hair. The jacket had a peplum, was fitted to her shape, and had white buttons. I really admired it. I used to stand by the fence to watch her go by." Lucille smiled at the memory of herself in the late 1920s standing in their Laramie yard to watch their beautiful, wealthy neighbor walk along the street.

"Mrs. Stickney would look at me and walk on. One day she said, 'Girls should not wear overalls.' Of course I knew that, but it's all I had to wear."

The young, fatherless Glenn children lived next door to Martha Stickney with their mother and grandparents. Lucille's grandfather, Peter Smart, was manager of the Old Kuster Hotel Saloon. Her mother worked in a candy kitchen uptown.

It apparently never occurred to their wealthy neighbor to help Mrs. Glenn and her fatherless children. The pre-teen girls and boys would probably have been thrilled to receive hand-me-down dresses and shirts from Mrs. Stickney.

Martha Wells Stickney had never known need or want. Born at Fillmore, Missouri, in 1842, Martha was one of three children of well-to-do parents. She was educated in a time when it wasn't necessary that a girl be taught anything other than getting married, settling down to homemaking and pleasing her husband.

Martha seemed to be of an adventurous turn of mind. She was first married at age nineteen in 1861. Her husband, Warner H. Terrell, was said to be a riverboat gambler. There is a hint that he was shot at a gaming table. Whether true or not, he died in August 1867. They had no children.

Martha's second marriage was to a Colonel Robert Conover, an officer in the Confederate Army and later sheriff of Andrew County, Missouri. He died in 1873.

That marriage may not have been a happy one for Martha resumed her former name of Terrell. The 1880 Census of Albany County, Dakota Territory [now Wyoming] reports she had two sons: Charles W., born in 1869, and Burleigh, born in 1871. They did not use their father's name, but went by the name of Terrell.

When and where Martha first crossed paths with widower Charles Bramel of Laramie, Wyoming, is not known. The two were married October 1, 1879, in Savannah, Missouri.

Martha and her young sons came to Laramie with her third husband. Bramel's young wife, Mary Jane, had died the year before, so Martha assumed the role of stepmother to the Bramel children, as well as bride to Charles.

≪∞ *Martha Stickney an attractive, very proper lady was also an astute businesswoman.* (Beery Collection)

Charles Bramel was a respected attorney in the frontier community, and the couple moved in the higher social circles of Laramie City. They were active in the Methodist Episcopal Church and several benevolent organizations.

Bramel was temperamental and had a drinking problem which the correct Martha found hard to tolerate. It is certain that she kept every rule of Victorian etiquette.

Item: "A lady isn't a lady unless her bed is made before noon."

Martha was up and busy early in the day.

Item: "Hat and gloves are proper street wear."

Little Lucille Glenn attested to that in the late 1920s.

Item: "A lady is modestly and properly dressed for any occasion."

Again Lucille Glenn would agree Martha was in adherence.

Item: "A lady's calling card is held in plain sight with the added confection of a lace-edged handkerchief held as background to the case."

This was especially important if the card-case was a petit-point affair or one of the latest, popular papier-mache models with an elegant painted surface.

The "at-homes" in Laramie were strictly observed and reported, sometimes in great detail, in the social columns of the newspapers. A proper Laramie woman announced certain days and times when she would be at-home and accepting callers. Friends were expected to make calls and to follow formal etiquette.

People with money were given much attention and Martha had plenty of money. Another plus was the popularity of Charles W. Bramel. The couple were busy with his and her children and their social obligations.

A lively business mind dwelt under Martha's shining hair-do. She loaned money at good interest. Borrowers did not always have cash at hand when a note fell due, and Martha seldom waited but pressed for payment. If it was not immediately forthcoming, the note was seldom renewed. This way she became the owner of a number of choice properties in town and in the country, a fact quite unusual in that day. The Women's Suffrage Act of 1870 declared women in Wyoming could legally own property and keep the money they earned. Still it was a surprise when they did.

Many debtors found it expedient to borrow elsewhere to keep their assets from Martha's eager hands. Some applicants had already borrowed to their limit, and the lady Shylock did not hesitate to foreclose.

One astute lady out-maneuvered Martha and so kept her choice bit of real estate. Sarah Montgomery operated her boarding house on the street now known as the Old Ivinson Block and at the site where the Frame Plant now operates. When her note came due, Sarah went at once to Ulrike Trabing and borrowed enough money to satisfy Martha's claim.

Martha's shylocking activities in no way affected her social standing. It may have added an aura of glamour to her mystique. Public recognition of businesswomen seemed to be growing, even engendering a measure of respect, if not awe, for the "little woman."

One of the longest-running and most interesting foreclosure proceedings was against a ranchwoman, Mary S. Daugherty.

MARY: PETTICOAT RANCHER

MARY'S WAS NOT a pampered life. Due to long years of toil and hardship she looked years older than Martha Stickney, rather than five years her junior.

Mary was a lady, even though her bed may not have always been made before noon. When she went out of the house she wore a sunbonnet and canvas work gloves. Instead of calling cards, she carried a hoe or pitchfork, a bucket of chicken feed or a milk pail.

Her "at homes" meant baking bread or cornbread, bending over a washtub and scrub board or wielding the homemade straw broom.

Mary, beloved by her neighbors for her cheerful and prompt response in times of illness, accident or birthing, did not excite envy through her wardrobe.

Mary had served in the Bandage Department of the Nurses' Corps during the Civil War. In 1863, she went into employ of Doctor George Frazer as his assistant and possibly as nanny for the Frazer children. When Frazer moved to Bannock City, Montana, Mary went along. When Frazer left the gold-mining camp for Mexico, Mary went too.

The trip south took them through Dakota Territory, and they stopped for a short time at Fort Sanders. Mary liked what she saw of the wide-sweeping Laramie Plains.

In Mexico, Mary met John Luber, another Civil War veteran, and they were married. In 1872, they moved to Wyoming and settled on Dutton Creek northwest of Laramie City. They operated a sheep ranch.

In 1876, Mary's life was changed forever. When her husband had not come home in the evening with the band of sheep, Mary became worried and set out to look for him.

All through the long, windy night, she conducted her desperate search and, in the early morning hours, found herself at the homestead of the Castidy family on Cooper Creek.

She hurried to the cabin, calling for help.

"We had seen Indians the day before," a member of the Castidy family related in later years. "And a traveler had stopped to tell our father he had seen a dead man at Dutton Creek crossing. The man had been scalped, his shirt stripped from his body and three knife slashes made on his back.

"Mr. Fuller, our father's partner, at once saddled a horse and set out for the creek. He soon returned, his horse all sweaty and lathered from the hard run. Mr. Fuller said the dead man was John Luber who lived about four miles northwest of us.

"During that long fear-filled night, the men made lead bullets to be prepared in case those Indians came our way. Just before dawn we heard a cry and saw a horrible apparition at the window. A dark, sun-browned face with windblown braided black hair, without a hat, protruding teeth in the distorted mouth—of course we were petrified with fear. Then someone realized that it was no Indian. It was Mrs. Luber, our young neighbor, hysterical from her long, dark night's search for her husband. She had made that terrible journey in the

∞ Mary and her second husband James Daugherty were happy together until his death. (Laramie Plains Museum)

dark afoot. No telling how many miles she had traveled. As gently as possible she was told what had happened. At daybreak the men went out and brought the man's body to the ranch. While the men dug a grave, the ladies prepared the body for burial. Mary made a covering for the bloody scalped head. She said she couldn't bear to think of John meeting his Maker without a covering for his naked head. She called it a Judgment Cap."

Her husband was buried on the Castidy ranch. The children outlined the grave with rocks and put a marker at the head.

So Mary was left alone. How she managed during the next three years is not clear. Nor is it clear when she met and decided to marry crotchety old sheepman James Daugherty.

They were married in 1879 and moved to his ranch on the Little Laramie River north of Sheep Mountain.

On December 4, 1886, Mary borrowed money from Martha E. Bramel and bought young cattle. When the note came due, she could not pay. Cattle prices were at a low point; selling off the cattle, including the increase, would not cover the principal, let alone the interest. Mary asked to renew the note. Martha reluctantly agreed. The note was renewed for one year in December 1888.

But on February 1, 1889, Martha initiated foreclosure proceedings. Every week for four months the Chattel Sale notice was published in the newspaper. Every two weeks in sunny or cold weather, over snowy or rutted roads, Martha drove her fine single-horse buggy out to the Daugherty ranch.

If she did enter the house, she would have seen a typical pioneer home, a two-room log cabin, rudely furnished, probably. There may have been hand-braided rag rugs on the floor, maybe geraniums blooming in the deep-set windows, and possibly a few treasured books.

Martha may have waited inside the cabin for the buyers to gather, for the auctioneer to come, for bidding to begin. Each week was the same. There may have been a large group of people, but there were no bids. The sale was postponed.

This continued for four months. At last Martha struck a bargain. She would take a plot of land to satisfy the $665.85 mortgage. She acquired the land. James and Mary Daugherty moved to another section of land they owned and continued their ranching operations.

During this time Martha had instituted divorce proceedings against attorney Charles W. Bramel citing drunkenness as cause. Charles, she charged, did "...disregard his marital duties toward this plaintiff and was an habitual drunkard... totally incompetent to transact ordinary business affairs...."

The divorce was granted in 1890. Shortly afterward Bramel went on a lecture circuit warning the public of the evils of drink.

Martha had engaged the services of Attorney S.W. Downey to replace Bramel as her legal council. It was in Downey's office that she met Darryl Stickney.

D.N. Stickney, a Canadian, ex-schoolmaster, member of the first legislature for statehood of Wyoming, was studying law with Downey. He and the lovely, wealthy 52-year-old divorcee were married in Colorado Springs in June 1893. They spent their honeymoon at the Chicago World's Fair.

*

Mary and Daugherty continued their ranching until, in 1916, James announced he was tired and wanted a rest. Mary wanted a rest, too. They sold their ranch and moved into Laramie to a house they bought on South Fourth Street.

Daugherty whittled and joined other old-timers in reminiscing about the old days. Mary, who had been satisfied to spend months at a time without ever coming to town, now found herself enjoying her neighbors and several social activities.

In the spring of 1918 rugged old James Daugherty died at his home after eating a hearty lunch. For nearly a year he had been troubled with severe stomach and heart problems. His end was sudden and a great shock to Mary. She fainted when told and for hours was in serious condition at their home.

Mary lived until 1924.

Martha Stickney lost her husband in 1913 after he underwent surgery. So she and Mary were both widowed. Mary lost two husbands. Martha outlived four husbands. Martha died at her home on South Seventh Street at age ninety.

∞

BIBLIOGRAPHICAL ESSAY. Albany County records at the County Courthouse furnished details involving ownership of properties of Martha Bramel-Stickney as well as property owned by Mary Luber Daugherty and James Daugherty.

The Albany County Library and the Laramie Plains Museum were further sources, with information from Greenhill Cemetery records. Details on their early personal lives were found in their obituaries. Other details were found in the *Laramie Sentinel, Laramie Republican,* and *Laramie Republican-Boomerang.*

Mildred Wood of Laramie, whose family lived in the Cooper Creek area, introduced me to Margaret Hayden of Evergreen, Colorado, a great-granddaughter of the homesteader Castidy. The tale of the Judgment Cap came from the Castidys.

Advertisements of the Chattel Sale told the story of the no-bid auctions. This device was used at times to allow a mortgager time to recoup finances in order to pay off the mortgage, or at other times when friends of the debtor felt foreclosure proceedings were ill-timed or unfair.

✤ A Grave Matter

I N THE BEGINNING, Laramie's first cemetery was "away out on the prairie thoroughly out of the way," according to James H. Hayford, editor of the city's *Daily Sentinel.* The town seemed destined to grow parallel to the railroad and never extend too far eastward. But things changed.

The town expanded. The East Side School was built on the block south of the cemetery, and many of the more affluent citizens began building in the vicinity—anything to get away from the noisy nightlife of the town's front streets.

The Union Pacific Railway Company owned the site of the graveyard. With the agitation for new home sites, the railroad company decided to sell the cemetery property as residential lots, so they asked the city fathers for help in relocating the cemetery.

Hayford, ever a booster for the "Gem City," advocated the move in his *Sentinel* and suggested the county's plentiful "boarders" at the city and county jails be put to work on the project and while they were at it, "...they might as well move those other graves scattered about town."

In those first days of the city, numerous deceased were planted more or less where they fell, or maybe in the one or two Boot Hills outside of town or in their own backyards, or in a hidden spot—like beneath a building if the dead was victim of a gunman. Additional graves lined the emigrant trail south of town.

Officials considered the relocation proposal and agreed with the railroad men. In May 1873, Sheriff Tom Dayton and the county and city prisoners took on the job of removal. Several townsmen aided in the work. One of the teamsters was "Old Jim" Sherrod, spinner-of-tales par excellence.

Sherrod tells of the raising: "We moved forty-two caskets to the new grounds and planted them over there. One of the caskets was so heavy it was about all four big husky men could do to lift it. It surely weighed 800 pounds or more.

"Curious…we pried it open. The body lay face down and it had turned to stone of a curious blue color. We knew the man. It was a young lawyer named Kerr who had come out from the East a few years before. He was a large man, over six feet tall, weighing around two hundred pounds and was in full flesh when he was buried."

Elias L. Kerr was a man of fine physique, a graduate of Yale and competent in legal matters. He was among the first-footers in Laramie City and opened his law office in 1868. Being of "…amiable nature, fine talents and good education" he quickly became a part of the better element of the rough end-of-track town.

According to the *Sentinel,* he "spoke firmly on the side of truth, right and justice, and cast his influence with those seeking to advance the community interest and welfare." In other words, he was a member of the famous vigilance committee when it became necessary to clean up the town in the fall of 1868.

Kerr served on the committee to organize the Library and Literary Association and was named as its first treasurer. He was one of the group which established the Union Presbyterian Church in May 1870 and was selected as a trustee on the first board.

He participated in the sporting events of the frontier town, served as president of the baseball club and ran in the frequent footraces, an attraction of merit for firemen.

Kerr was a popular figure at parties and dances and a welcome part of the social scene of Laramie and Fort Sanders. An articulate member of the bar.... A promising lawyer....

He was a drunkard....

On September 24, 1871, Elias Kerr became ill of what was first thought to be flu and a doctor was summoned. The doctor diagnosed not flu but *delirium tremens,* gave him medication and left medicine on the table beside the bed.

About 7 P.M. friends dropped in to see how he was and found Kerr dead in bed.

This unexpected turn caused a coroner's jury to at once convene to investigate the cause of the mysterious demise. The verdict was "death from an overdose of opium administered by himself whether with suicidal intent or not...."

He was buried September 26 in the city cemetery.

So, in 1873, the cemetery removal committee puzzled over their singular discovery and discussed the man's unexpected passing only little more than a year earlier.

Sherrod's story continues:

"Instead of lying on his back with hands crossed as is usual, he was turned over. He didn't look any different than when we buried him, except that he had turned to blue stone. I whetted my pocket knife on, the thigh and put a fine keen edge on it. It couldn't have been a chemistry in the soil that caused that change, for there were graves on all sides...we opened other caskets...his was the only one showing signs of petrification [*sic*].

"Of course we remembered and talked over the circumstances of his death...that in his delirium he may have taken too much medicine.

"We remembered, too, that the fellow had been sweet on the doctor's daughter, and the old man objected. We speculated about that...and speculated that the combination of booze and drug had caused the petrification and the strange color of the corpse.

"Looking at the stone body and at the way it lay we figured that Kerr must have been in a trance or under the influence of a powerful drug when he was buried and come to and turned over."

In those days coma often went undetected and living persons were mistakenly buried. Had this young man been buried alive and turned over in his struggle for air?

Had Kerr mistakenly taken too much medicine to alleviate his headache and could the combination of alcohol and drug have caused the chemical change? Was the dosage left on the table too strong in the first place?

Is it possible for a body, buried a little more than a year, to appear petrified and to look like blue stone? Or was Old Jim Sherrod just spinning another tale?

These grave questions will never be answered for the mystery doesn't end there.

When the site of the University of Wyoming was selected in 1886, it was necessary once again to relocate the city cemetery. So a second raising of bodies occurred.

Caskets from the first cemetery as well as those that had been added during the 1873-1886 years were disinterred and moved to the new location a quarter-mile north.

Many of the graves transferred from their original burial site had apparently been placed in the second cemetery with little or no record made of names, dates or plot locations— or if records were made, they had become lost. Wooden markers had fallen into decay or weathered to illegibility. Wood burial-boxes decayed, losing forever many identities.

With so many removals, it is even possible that boxes and identities were mixed-up.

As occurred in the first moving experience, an unknown number of graves were missed in the second transplanting to the new cemetery (Greenhill) for, in 1912 and 1940 during excavations for campus construction, rotted caskets and skeletons were found. Identification was impossible at that late date.

There is no clear record at Greenhill Cemetery of the number of caskets transferred there from the second graveyard. There is no record of Elias L. Kerr, and no mention of any date nor of a heavy casket.

The final resting place of Elias L. Kerr remains as much a haunting mystery as does his death.

Does he lie peacefully under another's marker or in an unmarked grave in Greenhill Cemetery? Or does he lie somewhere beneath the busy campus of Wyoming's University?

∞

BIBLIOGRAPHICAL ESSAY. Sources for this eerie tale are Laramie's *Daily Sentinel*, County Coroner's Records, Greenhill Cemetery Records, and the Clarice Whittenberg Collection at the American Heritage Center at the University of Wyoming.

꙳ ꙳ ꙳ ꙳ ꙳ ꙳ ꙳ ꙳ ꙳ ꙳ ꙳ ꙳ ꙳ ꙳ ꙳

THE OLD TIMER TELLS US HOW WOLVES LIKE "DOG SALMON." HE SAYS WOLVES GO TO THE MOUTH OF THE STREAM AND CHASE ALL THE SALMON UPSTREAM. WHEN THE WHOLE RUN IS AT THE HEAD OF THE STREAM, THE WOLVES SPOON THEM OUT WITH THEIR PAWS AND EAT THEM. THE BONES AREN'T DIGESTIBLE AND FIRST THING THE WOLF KNOWS THE BONES ARE STICKING OUT OF HIM IN ALL DIRECTIONS, AND THE WOLF LOOKS LIKE AN OLD FASHIONED CARDING MACHINE. THE OLD TIMER SAYS A GREAT MANY WOLVES HAVE LOST THEIR LIVES FOR NOT PICKING THE BONES OUT OF THEIR FISH.

꙳ ꙳ ꙳ ꙳ ꙳ ꙳ ꙳ ꙳ ꙳ ꙳ ꙳ ꙳ ꙳ ꙳ ꙳

✀ ABOUT FACE

A T LAST HE WAS free! He stepped outside the gate of the prison stockade and drew a deep, satisfying breath. It was a new sensation—fresh, clean air that had never been breathed before. No more stinking, sweating smells of prisoners and no more listening to their whinings and curses.

He caught the scents of greening sage, the sweet-grass smell of rain-drenched earth blowing across his shoulder. He was no longer a number. He was Clark Pelton again, a free man with a pardon in his pocket. He was twenty-five and the date was May 6, 1882.

*

Young Pelton knew what he wanted at age seventeen, and it wasn't life on his parents' farm in Ohio. Even though he knew that farm would be his someday since he was an only child, he wanted a bigger, exciting life. He headed west where the land was open, the sky high, and bright adventure beckoned.

Instead of the adventures he had pictured, the unskilled young man had to settle for the same dreary jobs he had scorned back in Ohio. He worked mainly in the Chugwater-Laramie Peak area and south, along the Horse Creeks and Sybille Creek.

During his first winter, 1874, Clark and a buddy built a small log cabin in a canyon on the west side of the Laramie

Range, which was called the Black Hills at that time. The two youths trapped small animals, shot deer, antelope, cougars and bobcats, skinned them and sold their hides. They had all the meat they wanted to eat, but not enough money.

They worked for ranchers, and Pelton soon found himself adept at breaking horses. The challenge and wildness of that work appealed to some unknown side of the young man. His reckless skill and daredevil attitude became a subject of conversation and concern among those who knew him. Although they knew he was a reliable kid, this dark, wild side was in their thoughts.

One particular ride was remembered and told and retold. Even old-timers marveled at the daredevil kid who made that late afternoon ride.

"That horse was a real wild one and terrorized by having a saddle and bridle on, let alone being surrounded by people or having one on his back.

"Regular bronc riders cautioned the kid and gave him pointers on how to handle that wild cayuse. Pelton listened but kept a confident grin on his face.

"When he swung up into the saddle and gave a wild yell that critter just exploded. Pelton kept a tight rein, fanned the critter's ears and stuck in the saddle like a cocklebur. That bronc came uncorked and tried every trick known to horsedom. They all failed; the kid was not unseated. He stayed in the saddle and when that bronc buck-jumped down a steep, boulder-strewn bank we all thought both of them would wind up at the bottom, and there'd be two broken necks.

"Well, it didn't happen. The ravine was all shadowed by early evening, and we could follow the route that bronc took down the steep bank by the sparks from his hoofs striking rocks, and the rush of falling rock was nothing to the squeals of the horse and the wild yells of its rider.

∞ *Clark and Bertha Pelton fell in love and were married in December 1886.* (Courtesy Pelton Family)

"We all dashed down the bank after them, expecting the worst. At the bottom stood the bronc, head down, legs trembling, sides heaving and sweating like a butcher. Completely beat. And that cocky kid still in the saddle!"

Pelton and his partner then had plenty of work, their own cabin and enough to eat. But this wasn't the life they had dreamed of. At last, while on a drunken spree, they chose an easier way to get rich. They rode east and held up a passing stage on the Cheyenne-Deadwood Stagecoach Line. And they got away with it. That was the important thing! The challenge was out-guessing and out-riding the law. They kept it up.

There were many close scrapes and near captures, but that only added to the excitement and challenge. At last, Clark Pelton committed the act that haunted him the rest of his life. He murdered a man.

Agnes Wright Spring relates in her book about the stage-line that Clark Pelton shot and killed Adolph Cuny, "one of the earliest pioneers in Wyoming," at the Six-Mile Road Ranch in July 1877. Cuny ran the Three-Mile Road Ranch just below Fort Laramie. But it was at the Six-Mile Road Ranch where the killing occurred.

The deputy sheriff, an assistant, and Adolph Cuny of Three-Mile came to Six-Mile (which was located on the Deadwood Road) to investigate a triple holdup. They captured Pelton and Duncan Blackburn. While the deputy and his aide sought other gang men, Blackburn and Pelton were left with Cuny. What actually transpired between them isn't mentioned in Spring's book, but Pelton, alias Billy Webster, alias The Kid, shot and killed Cuny. The two outlaws fled. They separated. Pelton took up with another outlaw named Laughing Sam. They went to Iowa, were eventually captured and sentenced to prison—Sam to Rapid City in Dakota and Pelton to Stillwater, Minnesota, for one year. Upon Pelton's release in 1879, he was re-arrested and brought to Wyoming to stand trial for the killing of Cuny. For this exercise he was sentenced to four years in the Territorial Prison at Laramie City.

In those days, murder, while frowned upon, was not considered as serious a crime as horse stealing. The theft of a horse or team meant the difference between life and death for the owner. Pelton's crime then was considered manslaughter.

The whole experience, and the sight of his mother sitting in the courtroom all during his trial, shocked the kid back to sensibility. He had to admit an obligation to his parents, even though he had thought himself independent. He became a model prisoner with the resolve to bring no more heartache to his family. Regular visits from his mother, and the fact that his father had twice made trips from Ohio, afoot both ways since he didn't trust train travel, impressed young Pelton deeply.

While in prison, the young man took part in the religious services instituted and conducted by the warden's wife and members of the Christian community of the town.

Clark's mother had moved to Laramie from the family farm in Ohio when he first went on trial. When he was sentenced, she remained in the western town and began efforts through friends and the Baptist Church to have him released.

Such dedication and the devotion of his parents overwhelmed the youth with shame. He became a Christian and never deviated from that path.

Upon his pardon and release from prison, his mother urged him to return with her to Ohio.

"No, Mother," he told her. "I cannot. It was here I lost my good name, and I must stay here and redeem my reputation."

Reluctantly his mother agreed, and after a few years she returned east, proud of her only son and fully confident in his determination and ability to restore the name of Pelton to respectability.

Clark first worked as a brakeman on the Union Pacific Railroad. It was dangerous work, moving along car tops in all kinds of weather to set hand brakes. It was worse in wintertime when the wooden walkway was ice-covered or the wind swooped down from the mountains. Another hazard, often overlooked by brakees, was unexpectedly coming upon a snowshed and forgetting to duck.

The invention, by Westinghouse, of air brakes removed much danger for brakees. But young Pelton had already taken another job. When contractor-builder A.S. Blackburn offered him work, he took it. Pay was small, but it was honest work and safe. And he was free and trusted.

If ever Clark felt a longing to again ride the wide country in the old reckless, carefree way, he quashed it. No more prison for him! He did return to the little hideaway cabin in the canyon on occasion and enjoyed the sense of freedom and solitude. But he was now a townsman, and the trips were infrequent.

His first job with Blackburn was as carpenter at the new University of Wyoming's first building—soon called "Old Main."

His daughter Nellie tells of that job: "Dad was working on the platform in the auditorium. Somehow or other he put a knotty pine board right in the middle of the platform. Then he was sorry. For many years he couldn't go into that room without noticing that knot. How he wished he could replace it!"

He learned a lesson from that knot, though. Never again did he allow any shoddy work to be done by himself or any of the men he later employed.

After a time Pelton took employment with lumberyard owners Morrison and Merrill. Within a short time, he became foreman, and after a few years, was able to buy into the company. Through his work he met Bertha Thobro, the beautiful sister of Mrs. Merrill. They fell in love and were married in early December 1886.

When Clark became a Christian, he endeavored in every way to point out the evils of drink. The Temperance Movement was growing strongly in the country, and Pelton was asked to lecture on the subject. He made no pretense of having led a blameless life and referred to his early experiences openly as caution to reckless young blades. His sometimes emotional recitals aroused sympathy and often tears among his listeners. And when Clark expressed his determination to lead a better life, there was frequent applause. The community only needed to review the activities of this young man over the past few years to know he would reach his goal. Many a youth was inspired to sign the Temperance pledge by Pelton's example.

Pelton took over the Morrison-Merrill lumber business and became a contractor-builder with his own employees. His work was exemplary, and he was awarded many contracts.

He organized one of the first cooperatives in the state of Wyoming. The group was incorporated in 1891 under the company name Clark Pelton and Employees, Inc.

When Diana Herran Brown, pioneer widow of old-time freighter Jackson K. Brown, sold her homestead to Young and Wilkinson for a subdivision to the city, most of the building contracts were let to Pelton and Company.

He insisted on the finest work from his partners and they, being upright men, never disappointed him. The co-op gained the enviable reputation of high-class workmanship and seemed to never lack for work.

When the inevitable slowdown came in the building industry, Pelton set up a sawmill or two in the mountains that had always beckoned him. Summertimes he took his family to the mill-camp near the Colorado state line, and they enjoyed living in the magnificent trackless woods.

Pelton took on a coal dealership during the winter to increase income. He also set up a small grocery store. At that time, and for many years afterwards, small neighborhood stores graced the town, a convenience to residents who found it difficult to make the trip uptown, usually afoot. Pelton's first store was on Park Street.

Pelton at one time operated a used-furniture store and even, in later years, took a flier into the used-car business.

The Pelton's first baby, a boy, died of scarlet fever at the age of two months. Later there were two daughters, Nellie and Laura.

Nellie related in her memoir of her father that in 1904 Clark decided to return to Ohio and take over the family farm. He "found it too slow and brought us all back to Wyoming. Since he had sold all his business holdings to go back to Ohio, he became a partner in the Boston-Wyoming Lumber Company at Centennial and soon he was back in Laramie engaged in the work he most enjoyed—building. To this business he soon added another, house moving. He bought out W.H. Beaudoin. One of their first projects was to move and renovate the old Presbyterian Church and parsonage from their Third Street sites.

"Dad also liked spending much time in the mountains fishing," daughter Nellie wrote. "He located and filed on a claim and did placer mining on the creek that now bears his name. In his later years Dad got back into the grocery business. In 1928, he bought a two-story building and converted it to a combination home-grocery-hotel. It was one of the earlier buildings in town and had been built for Laramie jeweler and one-time mayor Louis Miller. It stood near the railroad tracks where the Pacific Power plant later stood" [presently the site of the Safeway Store on Second Street].

The old house had unusually heavy timbers as floor stringers. The lumber had been meant for special use on the railroad. Miller had obtained it and put it to his own use. When the first stockyards were built in that area, the house was moved to Third and Bradley and set up as a Stockmen's Hotel.

It was a commodious building offering six sleeping rooms on the second story, a welcome place for ranchers waiting to load out livestock for shipping.

Pelton operated this hotel and grocery until his death in 1930 while on a fishing trip along Pelton Creek. His passing was deeply mourned, for here was a man who had made a vow and kept it. He had conquered the dark side of his soul, redeemed the good name of Clark Pelton and left it among the most highly respected of his time.

∞

BIBLIOGRAPHICAL ESSAY. I consulted the usual sources of county records and newspapers of the day. Information gleaned from newssheets consisted of sensational tales of Pelton's youthful escapades. Later references dealt with advertisements, and some family items, such as trips to the mountains for picnics and fishing, which Pelton enjoyed heartily. Through the various advertisements, it was fairly easy to trace Pelton's advancement in business.

The *Annals of Wyoming* and Agnes Wright Spring's book *Cheyenne and Black Hills Stage and Express Route,* previously cited, gave more information on the outlaw years, as did some City Police Minutes (Laramie city records).

I wish to express special gratitude to Elnora Frye of Laramie who graciously shared her historical knowledge and whose in-depth research for her book, *Atlas of Wyoming Outlaws at the Territorial Penitentiary* (Laramie: Jelm Mountain Publications, 1990), was helpful in writing this story.

Pelton's about face and his straight-road life is found in records of the Baptist Church and his affiliation with some beneficent orders.

Memoirs left by daughter Nellie Pelton Allen, and a 1979 letter from daughter, Laura Pelton Geigley of California, added to the information. Grandchildren Bertha Allen Ward and Dr. Don Allen, both of Laramie, told of the cabin in a canyon in the Laramie Range. Dr. Allen related the tale of the wild bronc ride as told by a witness years ago.

As to the cabin: "It was moved to Laramie in the 1940s and set up in the 600 block of Bradley Street," Dr. Allen stated.

The cabin still stands at 613 Bradley. It is now covered with green-painted siding, a modest building, jealous of its secrets.

∽ ∽ ∽ ∽ ∽ ∽ ∽ ∽ ∽ ∽ ∽ ∽ ∽ ∽ ∽

IN AN ITEM IN THE FEBRUARY 1, 1890, *LARAMIE WEEKLY SENTINEL*, THE PRISONERS AT THE WYOMING PENITENTIARY COMPLAINED ABOUT HAVING TO WORK IN CONVICT LABOR:

"IT'S BAD ENOUGH BEING DEPRIVED OF OUR LIBERTY WITHOUT BEING COMPELLED TO WORK. IF WE HAD BEEN WILLING TO WORK FOR A LIVING WE WOULDN'T BE HERE. LET THOSE WORK WHO CAN'T LIVE BY THEIR WITS. WE ARE HONORED GUESTS OF THE STATE AND IT IS AN OUTRAGE THAT WE MUST BE COMPELLED TO WORK FOR OUR OWN SUPPORT."

∽ ∽ ∽ ∽ ∽ ∽ ∽ ∽ ∽ ∽ ∽ ∽ ∽ ∽ ∽

❧ THE WAG AND
THE PROSTITUTE

THE LADY COULD neither read nor write, and she may have seemed guileless and untutored, but Nettie Wright Stewart was sharp enough to survive several scrapes with the law.

Described as "a petite blonde with braided taffy-colored hair, wide blue eyes, a winsome smile and a soft pleasing Scandinavian accent," Nettie Stewart arrived in Buffalo, Wyoming Territory, from Laramie in the fall of 1879 and set up her house of pleasure.

Burton S. Hill relates in his tale "A Girl Called Nettie" that Nettie and a man named McLead jointly ran a saloon and parlor house in the building owned by Nettie. The drinking part was owned and operated by McLead. Nettie's parlors were at the back of the house. On December 21, 1881, she and McLead were visiting in one of her rooms when Bill Heaton, one of their bartenders, burst into the room, began a loud quarrel with McLead, and finally shot him. Nettie, who witnessed the event, apparently did not interfere nor immediately report the incident. Heaton had plenty of time to escape. He rode to Fort McKinney and asked the sentry at the gate to give him asylum in the post guardhouse.

Nettie was later charged on three counts. Two of the charges related to the shooting—accessory to the murder of

McLead and grand larceny in taking his gold ring and other effects. The third charge was a morals issue with a man named Jud Braziel. The pair was fined twenty-five dollars each.

On the first charges, Nettie was put under a four hundred dollar bond. Two prominent businessmen of Buffalo paid the bond, and Nettie was free to continue her public service.

Later, at the trial, Nettie was found not guilty of complicity in the murder of McLead. Heaton was out of the country by then, so the matter was dropped. Nettie was found equally innocent of stealing McLead's gold ring and other personal effects. She even wound up legally owning McLead's portion of their partnership.

She expanded her house and business in an elegant manner. She added a second story to her building. The main floor was used as barroom and dance hall. Upstairs were her private living quarters and entertainment rooms. Fine rugs, lace curtains and good furniture graced the rooms. A set of fine Dresden china dressed the table for her guests. She hired three "entertainers" and operated her parlor house in a decorous and genteel manner. Yes, Nettie's lifestyle improved with the death of her partner.

Nettie had made her first appearance in Wyoming Territory in Laramie. She was known in Laramie as both Nettie and Nellie Wright. She operated a pleasure house on Front Street called the Crystal Wine Parlors. It was the site of several questionable capers in the early 1870s, not too different from those in Buffalo.

She was well acquainted with the court system in Laramie. N.L. (Judge) Andrews, the wit and old practical joker of Laramie's first days, defended Nettie-Nellie on her frequent appearances in Laramie city court on charges of "keeping a house of ill repute," and like accusations. Andrews usually got her off—with the least possible fines.

On December 4, 1876, in Laramie city court one Joseph Wilson was arrested and tried for stealing $160 from "keeper" Pawnee Liz. Edward Cunningham and Nettie Wright were called as witnesses. Joe was found not guilty, but was fined five dollars anyway for his frolic with Liz. A few days later Nettie was tried for larceny involving a prized knife.

Judge N. L. Andrews presided at the trial. Nettie pleaded not guilty. Andrews dismissed the case and "the knife was returned to the owner."

That same day (December 8, 1876), the sympathetic Judge Andrews performed the marriage ceremony for Mrs. Nellie Wright, age 23, and Mr. John (Jack) Davis, age 39.

Marriage didn't affect her business activities one whit. It appears that husband Jack joined wholeheartedly in the enterprise, for he was soon hauled in and fined for "keeping." He was released, of course.

The following March there was a great to-do in town. It was payday at Fort Sanders and most of the money was blown in Laramie's numerous pleasure houses. Fifty-seven soldiers, nursing black eyes, bloody noses and hangovers were arrested and thrown into the guardhouse at the fort. A general court-martial was held. No censure of the houses or saloons in town was mentioned.

A Saturday night celebration at Nellie-Nettie's wine parlors, in late April 1877, ended in a shooting.

Two lawmen from Greeley, Colorado, William C. Mullion and Richard Davis, went to the pleasure house of Nettie-Nellie "looking for a criminal wanted in Colorado." Mullion became involved in an argument with an associate of a man named William Schnell.

Mullion removed his coat to fight, handing the coat to Schnell. Schnell began rifling the coat pockets, and Officer Davis ordered him to stop. Schnell removed Mullion's

∞ *Judge N.L. Andrews, a prominent man in Laramie, was a wit, practical joker and a friend of Nettie Wright.* (Jim Gatchell Museum)

pocketbook and ran. Davis and Mullion went after him, shooting and yelling "Stop! Stop!" Schnell was hit as he ran outside and down the alley. He fell, but got up and ran again, disappearing into the darkness. He was later found in the rail-yards, dead, with four bullets in him. Davis and Mullion were taken in for questioning on the fracas. Since they proved they were on official business, they were released.

The newspaper reported that the affair had occurred in Nettie's "bagnio." She flew into a rage, declaring she "didn't keep no bagnio nor any other kind of house, only an old invalid man who pays for his care and keep."

So Nettie was not responsible for disturbing the peace that night. Nor was she at fault in February 1879 when May

Howard, a Cheyenne prostitute, was visiting the wine parlors and was shot dead. Nettie was found to be a friend of May and wholly free of blame in the tragedy. Texas Jim, who shot the girl, claimed it was an accident, and he was "honorably acquitted."

No record in Albany County shows how, when or where Nellie-Nettie shed husband Jack Davis, but in the fall of 1879 she left Laramie and went to Buffalo where her friend N.L. Andrews had moved. She promptly called on him, asking his help in collecting on a $250 check. He obliged, and she settled down to conducting her business in the town.

Nettie made the acquaintance of the soldiers and officers at Fort McKinney, which was three miles west of Buffalo. She was soon arrested at Fort McKinney with two soldiers, Starr and Blackwood, for stealing government arms and ammunition. The trio were taken to Laramie City and locked up in the territorial prison.

The *Laramie Sentinel* reported that U.S. Marshal Schnitger was elated because he had a woman prisoner. Nettie was the first woman to be housed in the Territorial Prison.

"The lady claims to have been an old resident of Laramie," the *Sentinel* reported, "...[she was] one of the martyrs driven from here by the bigotry and intolerance of our Women's Grand Jury."

The *Sentinel* should have known better.

Women served as jurors only in the spring court sessions of 1870 and 1871, and in the fall of 1870. Nettie was not driven out of Laramie by a grand jury composed of women since she was much in evidence there until 1879. Eight years is quite a while to take a hint.

The trial for the Fort McKinney affair was held in Laramie. Nettie gave the names of Laramie old-timers as character references—Ira Pease, N.L. Andrews, and other prominent Laramie men.

Andrews, of course, was married and a happy family man. He had settled into business in Buffalo, and it may be the appearance of Nettie in that town was not too welcome. He apparently had little to do with the winsome blonde after they both moved to Buffalo.

This may have irritated the lady and prompted her to advertise their earlier acquaintance in Laramie during the Fort McKinney court proceedings.

The trials of Nettie and the soldiers were held separately in the Laramie court. The jury was composed of longtime residents of Laramie. In her pleasing Scandinavian accent, Nettie made discreet mention of her friendships with well-connected Laramie men. What was any old-timer to do but find the petite blonde innocent?

So Nettie returned to Buffalo and resumed her business. Then came the unfortunate incident with McLead which left Nettie both innocent and more wealthy.

It appears that the townsmen of Laramie and Buffalo were completely snookered by the little untutored lady who could neither read nor write.

∾

BIBLIOGRAPHICAL ESSAY. Laramie city records, Albany County records, and District Court records provided information.

Most of the information concerning Nettie's activities at Buffalo comes from Burton S. Hill's tale "A Girl Called Nettie" which appeared in the *Annals of Wyoming* (October 1965).

Some of the information about Nettie at Buffalo is open to question since Nettie-Nellie was in Laramie about 1875, definitely in 1876. There is much similarity in the conduct of the lady in Laramie and at Buffalo. Any good ploy usually works well more than once.

✠ KATIE

"I WAS IN THE Trabing store in Medicine Bow when a little girl walked into their lives," Alice Mathews Shields related in an interview in the *Annals of Wyoming.* "Gus Trabing and his wife had no children of their own. A miner from old Carbon, a coal mining town southwest of Medicine Bow, came into the store holding the little girl by the hand. 'Howdy,' he said to Mr. Trabing. 'You got any children?' Mr. Trabing told him no. The man said, 'I'll trade you this little girl for a sack of flour. My wife died and left me with seven.'

"Gus Trabing thought he was joking, but when he saw he was in earnest, he called Mrs. Trabing and they agreed to the trade. The man took his sack of flour, threw it on the load of potatoes and drove off. He never looked back. The little girl, blond, and not unlike the Trabings, stood with her hand shading her eyes and watched him out of sight. She did not cry and never uttered a word. I couldn't understand the actions of any of them.

"The Trabings were very good to the little girl and when she was old enough to go to school, they moved to Laramie City and gave her a good education. They named her Mable. She became a grand singer and sang 50 years ago in the Tabor Opera House in Denver. Mable married one of the Swan boys of the Swan Livestock Company. They parted years later, and she kept on with her singing for several years."

∞ *Gus and Ulrike Trabing traded a sack of flour for Katie when she was eleven years old.* (Courtesy Trabing Family)

So begins the tale of the lovely, talented girl who became known as Trabing's daughter. Mrs. Shields story contains errors.

The little girl was eleven years old, and her name was Kathryn Skoglund, not Mable. Two of her sisters lived in the area. Four years later the 1880 census reported Annie, age twenty-nine, was married to John Ward and lived at the Ward Road Ranch, an overnight stop for the Trabing Brothers freight wagons between Medicine Bow and the far northern reaches of Wyoming and Montana. The other sister, Margaret, called Maggie, was married to George Powell, a rancher in the valley of LaPrele Creek. Maggie was twenty-two, according to the 1880 census, and Katie was fifteen that year. She was listed with both sisters in that population count, by different enumerators. One brother, John, age twenty-seven, was a freighter and may have worked for the Trabing line. Others of the family may have lived in Iowa where the family resided before coming to Wyoming.

No record has been found that August and Ulrike Trabing adopted Katie, but she was definitely taken as a member of the family and given every advantage Gus later gave to his own children. This warm inclusion and acceptance of the little girl and the real affection was enough to dispel any feeling of unworthiness Katie may have felt from her father's abandonment. This, and other friendships the child formed, must have fulfilled the human need to feel precious to someone.

One of those friendships was forged in those early days at Medicine Bow. John J. Clarke, young teenaged telegrapher for the Union Pacific Railroad Company, was just at the right age to accept a little girl's interest and shy friendship. Clarke was quite homesick for his family far in the East, and the Trabings took a deep interest in his welfare, too. This, of course, led to a sort of brother-sister relationship that lasted well into the 1920s, even though they were far separated by then.

When Johanna Raduchal arrived from Wisconsin to visit her half-sister Ulrike and August, she and Katie became close friends. Later, Ulrike divorced August so that he might marry Hannah. Hannah and Gus had maintained a long time extra-marital relationship and Gus had fathered their two children. Then Katie spent part of her time with sisters Annie and Margaret. This accounts for her being counted twice in the 1880 census. Katie also spent time living in Laramie with Ulrike, until Ulrike married John Hill and they moved to Omaha. Katie was also close to August and Hannah and their children, George and Mable, and lived with them on occasion.

The loving relationship between the children is shown in the inscription on a photograph Katie sent to George in the late 1890s: "From Your Loving Friend, Kathryn Skoglund."

Since the Trabings were well known all over the north country, the name proved helpful to the orphan girl. She attended school in Laramie City while Gus and his brother Charles still operated their famous freight-line out of Medicine Bow. The daily trip was probably made by train, for the brothers both lived in the Bow, even though there was an outfitting store in Laramie, operated by Trabing employees. It may be that Gus or Charles made the train trip frequently with the young girl, to oversee business while she attended school.

Katie was an apt student, and it was immediately apparent that she was also blessed with an exceptional singing voice. Numerous accounts appear in the Laramie newspapers of a school event in which the "splendid voice of Katie Trabing" added to the program. "KATIE TRABING IS RECOGNIZED STAR OF THE EVENING" headlined one newspaper article. Her academic ability was also given much praise. For a waif abandoned by her father, the lovely young girl was doing well.

August Trabing liked to tell in later years of his appearances on the vaudeville stage in their old Blue Front National Theatre, and later in the Mannerchor Group as a singing comedian. It may be that he helped Katie overcome her early shyness, for her singing talent was well developed, as Mrs. Shields mentioned, and she became a fine professional singer.

Trabing's connections in Cheyenne may have influenced the appointment of Katie as a transcriber in the office of Surveyor-General David, father-in-law to Governor Carey.

In this office, Katie developed another deep and long-lasting friendship, this with another young worker in the David office named Grace Hebard.

Miss Hebard made a praiseworthy niche for herself in the field of education at the University of Wyoming, as a historian of note, and as one of the few women with a degree in law at that time. Dr. Hebard wrote a number of treatises and books on Wyoming history and other academic subjects which attracted national attention.

Katie's years in Cheyenne led to her close friendship with Louisa Swan, daughter of Alexander Swan of the Swan Land and Livestock Company. It also brought her to the romantic attention of young William Swan, just three years older than Katie. Their romance blossomed, and Katie was invited to make the Grand Tour with Mrs. Swan, Will and Louisa.

The Grand Tour was required of all young debutantes about to enter into the formal social scene. Wyoming may have been on the edge of nowhere, but the more affluent resident made many trips east, attended fashionable soirees, and were as up to the minute as anyone of the accepted 400 in the East. Louisa and Katie, then, were "finished" debutantes and could take their places in the Cheyenne social scene.

Katie's talent was also recognized in Cheyenne. She sang with the Episcopal Choir in Cheyenne and at the City Opera House. Each of her appearances was greeted with utmost praise. Whenever she sang, she was the featured performer.

Katie and Will Swan were married. No record has been found to date their marriage, so the legend of their marriage in England may be true. The Swans were of Scottish ancestry, and the ceremony may have been performed with the Scottish relatives in attendance.

Will and Katie may have lived in Cheyenne. The Trabing nemesis, fire, destroyed all records the family at Laramie had kept. Their later years must be pieced together from haphazard items gleaned elsewhere.

John J. Clarke's correspondence with Dr. Grace Hebard tells of encountering Katie in Kansas City in 1910, Los Angeles in 1929, and hearing of her stage adventures during the days since Medicine Bow. Mrs. Shield's statement that the girl sang in the Tabor Theatre in Denver is evidently correct. It seems she appeared on stage in Central City's Opera House before going east to Chicago and Kansas City. However, no records have been found which identify productions she performed in. It is possible that she used a stage name.

There is some question as to what happened to Will Swan.

One source has it that Katie and Swan were divorced; another that he died in the crash of a troop train in Tupelo, Mississippi, when headed for the Cuban campaign with Teddy Roosevelt's Rough Riders. Or he may have died of malaria in the Philippines in that same war with Spain. It is known that Katie was married to a man name Hammond and lived in Kansas City during the last months of her life.

She had fallen and fractured her hip, and since she was then in frail health, she never recovered from that mishap. Katie's daughter, Louisa Swan Thale was with her during those last bed-ridden months.

∞

BIBLIOGRAPHICAL ESSAY. The Daily and Weekly *Sentinels* were only mildly helpful in regard to Katie Trabing's adventures. Most references were found in the *Annals of Wyoming* (Fall 1941).

A letter from Dr. Grace Raymond Hebard to the editor of the *Cheyenne Tribune* gives details of Katie's life and touches on her career. There was no mention of Mr. Swan, except the marriage.

John J. Clarke's letter to Dr. Hebard, informing her of Katie's death, was another source. He sketched a bit of Katie's career as included in the story.

Mention was made in the *Boomerang* of March 21, 1899, that Katie sang in a duet with a Miss Gillum at the Cheyenne Opera House. "Katie's soprano was perfect."

✥ WALK A CROOKED MILE

One of the prisoners over in the Pen puts in a portion of his time making jewelry. Abalone and other materials is set on dimes and quarters and formed into handsome pins, buttons and sleeve buttons. The man has a family in our midst dependent on him for support and those who visit [the Pen] should hunt him up and see what he can do for them in his line.

Laramie Daily Sentinel
March 2, 1877

THE MAN WAS AN ENGLISHMAN named Edward Frodsham. He was known for his skill with jewelry and for his explosive temper.

It wasn't long before Laramie's citizens learned what Frodsham could do for them in both lines.

Edward Frodsham was serving time for "assassinating" a man in Evanston, Wyoming. The story from Evanston said there was no assassination. It was a fair fight. The man, Peasely, "was a mean, worthless gambler and pimp who had insulted Frodsham and his wife beyond endurance. Peasely was advancing on Frodsham with a deadly weapon and Frodsham shot him." The general opinion at Evanston was that it was a good deed. The man needed killing.

Edward Frodsham's attractive wife saw to it that his time in the Wyoming Territorial Penitentiary was brief. (Beery Collection)

Mrs. Frodsham, who was said to be a cousin or niece of her husband and still in her teens, possessed such beauty of face and figure as to arouse protective instincts on all sides. The fact that Margaret Frodsham took in washing to support their children proved to be another great asset to Frodsham in his troubles. She got up a petition asking that Frodsham be pardoned and took it around Evanston, Laramie and Cheyenne and obtained several hundred signatures of the most prominent men of those towns.

Margaret's youth and beauty lent glamour and an aura of knight-protecting-a-lady's-honor to the shooting, and it touched the sensitive hearts of all the gallant men who gladly signed the petition.

The attorney for the prosecution signed, as did the judge who heard the case. Supreme Court Judges Thomas, White and Pease, and the Delegate to the Territorial Congress and Speaker of the Legislature, N.L. Andrews of Laramie, all signed the petition. They wrote personal letters to Governor Thayer, to Secretary French and Judge Peck.

The Governor granted a pardon to Frodsham which touched off a blast of publicity and protest. The town of Evanston soothed the public brow by "finding no fault with the pardon." They repeated that the man Peasely deserved killing.

Edward Frodsham was freed on January 11, 1878, and exchanged his prison cell for a house in Laramie on A Street (present day Ivinson). He, his beautiful wife and children lived in the back rooms. The large front room served as his jewelry workshop, display area and workspace for his friend Eli Landers, a watch repairman.

The enterprise began most prosperously. Spring passed and summer arrived.

A quiet August day was interrupted by the racketing of pistol fire. Onlookers gathered at windows and doors to watch Frodsham and a Utah cattle dealer named Abraham Taylor chasing each other, dodging around a drugstore sign and shooting with intent to do bodily harm.

Taylor had gone to the house of Miss May Frost across the street from Frodsham's, seeking her sexual favors. A railroad tie worker named Roberts was in her parlor and refused to leave. After heated argument, Taylor put him out in the street.

A short time later Roberts returned accompanied by Frodsham. The men apparently were acquaintances, and their verbal exchange with Abraham Taylor became hot and ugly. The newcomers began to beat Taylor who still lay on the lady's bed. They knocked him to the floor, beating and kicking him unmercifully, then left the house. Miss Frost sympathetically treated Taylor's wounds.

Taylor went to his room at the Railroad Hotel and got his gun. Now armed, the cattle dealer went to the jewelry shop and called Frodsham out. They argued. Frodsham slapped Taylor's face, and Eli Landers handed his boss a gun yelling "Kill the son of a bitch!"

The two men began firing at each other, dodging around the signboard in an ungraceful, deadly dance.

Then Roberts moved in, kicking at Taylor, then tripping him. Frodsham began to pistol-whip the downed man, beating him about the head and shoulders while Eli Landers egged him on. Roberts continued kicking and Frodsham continued beating Taylor with his gun.

A passing soldier intervened, pulling the men away from the prostrate, bleeding Taylor. Someone had gone for the police, and lawmen arrived in time to arrest the combatants and Landers for his part in the affray.

The railroad tie worker Roberts and Eli Landers went to jail. Taylor was taken to his hotel room where Dr. Harris patched him up and expressed the hope that he would live. Frodsham was also patched up and allowed to remain in his home with his wife as nurse. All participants "expressed regret for the incident."

By August 22, the two men were reportedly "recovering nicely," and three weeks later, Edward Frodsham took Eli Lander's horse and skipped town during the night. Two days later his beautiful young wife sold her household goods and followed him, presumably to Denver.

It was well Frodsham left, for when his trial was pressed what defense did he have for attacking Taylor? There was no provocation as far Frodsham was concerned. And why did Roberts go to Frodsham for help? Were they old friends? Could any of the men justify their actions?

With the Frodshams gone, Laramie breathed a sigh of relief and shrugged off the embarrassment of having been so taken in by them.

However, the incident could not be easily forgotten. Another ruckus in town only days after the Frodshams left caught public attention.

First the man Roberts, also known as O'Brien, was caught trying to obtain goods under false pretenses. He was sentenced to a year in the penitentiary across the river.

Then two convicts were released from the pen, a William Enright, described as an accomplished thief and a hard character, and a man of kinder mold, James Magee.

The pair at once set about celebrating their freedom. They became loud and threatening, and Enright began to browbeat the bartender at J.J. Fein's City Brewery. Marshal Larry Fee and Policeman W.W. Butler were called and the two ex-cons were arrested. As they were being marched the three blocks to the county jail, Enright began a verbal abuse of Butler.

"You won't get away with this, you know. I'm gonna get you for it, you son of a bitch."

Butler pulled his gun to enforce the "law about to jail a prisoner." Enright pulled a pistol he had stolen earlier in the evening. Apparently he had not been searched since he was freshly out of prison and shouldn't have had time to acquire a gun. Butler's gun was stuck, would not discharge nor revolve. Enright cursed him and let loose a shot. Butler began to run toward the jail with the convict firing after him. Then the convict ran away in the darkness. Butler heard him leap the board fence surrounding a residence, flounder in the irrigation ditch, then pound on down the street toward town.

Butler dashed to the jail, obtained a gun, and accompanied by Night Watchman Donahue set out to find the escaped Enright.

They finally ran him aground in M.H. Murphy's Front Street saloon. At sight of Butler, Enright made as if to pull his gun from his coat pocket, and Butler shot him.

Investigation revealed that William Enright was really John Enright of Malone, New York. He had served seven years in the California State Prison along with Edward

Frodsham. Another of their pen pals was Eli Landers whose real name was Eli Lee.

This trio was active for years in California and Utah. Roberts, a shady character, whose real name was O'Brien, was well known to Denver police and apparently comfortable in fellowship with Frodsham and his cronies.

The horse Frodsham rode out of Laramie belonged to Landers/Lee and was kept in a pasture near town. It was trained to respond only to a peculiar whistle; authorities surmised the animal was used by Eli for night-time skullduggery.

They also suspected Frodsham and Roberts were involved, but manly sympathy for the shapely beauty of Mrs. Frodsham was so strong, authorities were reluctant to make accusations.

Of course, now with Enright dead, Roberts back in the penitentiary and Landers/Lee in custody of Utah officers on earlier charges of murder, and the Frodshams gone—there was no case.

The newspaper summed it up in one short comment: "We're glad to be rid of them."

More news of the Frodshams reached Laramie in late December.

In Leadville, Colorado, Edward Frodsham had pistol-whipped a former Laramie saloon-keeper named Peter Thams and shot him in the leg. No reason was given.

Thams was a "long-time citizen and businessman of Laramie, universally respected for his honorable dealings and genial character." When later Thams died, the *Sentinel* stated that the high-tempered Frodsham would in all probability stretch hemp.

But he didn't.

His lovely wife apparently again came to his rescue. It had worked very well once, why not again? She may have been a teenager, but Edward was a mature and ruthless thirty-seven. He was not averse to using the youth and beauty of his wife in another appeal to manly chivalry. And Margaret needed her husband, the father of her children and loyal provider. Manly chivalry would respond.

All was quiet with the Frodshams for a year and then Laramie heard again of their "incarnate devil."

The *Leadville Chronicle* reported that Edward Frodsham was in jail for lot-jumping. As a real estate dealer, his hand was heavy in the game of removing owners and claimants from choice lots and taking possession. The city lots were then sold for ripe sums, or if a claim was rich or the location promising in value, gang members kept it.

Finally greedy, sharp-witted Frodsham chose the wrong man to bully, or else he was losing his touch. The town of Leadville, tough as it was, had had enough of the gang's bunko antics—or, as was hinted, certain members of the city council, involved with the thieves, needed a scapegoat, and Edward Frodsham was it.

The Leadville paper related, "Around 2 o'clock at night, a party of seventy vigilantes went to Sheriff Watson's home, rousted him out of bed and drove him to the jail. They disarmed the deputy and forced the officers to open the cell. They took Frodsham and a foot-pad named Charles Stevens from the jail to an unfinished building where they hung them from a roof-beam."

Signs attached to Frodsham's body gave fearsome warning to all lot-jumpers in general.

The *Laramie Sentinel* commented: "Frodsham formerly lived here. He was a bad and dangerous man whose hands have been stained repeatedly with human blood...."

The city of Leadville was later "threatened with a $60,000 lawsuit for the lynching of Edward Frodsham, filed by Mrs. Frodsham, who is a niece of her husband. The legality of her marriage will doubtless be raised," reported an item in the December 20, 1879, *Sentinel.*

The legality of the marriage was doubtless raised. There was no suit. Mrs. Frodsham took her children and returned to her family in Utah.

A length of hemp put an end to the crooked trail of the ruthless, hot-tempered Frodsham and was said to have "brought law and order to Leadville."

∽

BIBLIOGRAPHICAL ESSAY.   Newspaper items as mentioned in the story appeared in the *Sentinel's* pages of 1877 through 1879.

The Frodshams were of the Mormon faith. Edward's father had two wives. Edward was a son of the first wife.

My gratitude to Gene Frodsham of Arizona, a descendent of the second marriage, for providing material to back up the story I have told, and for later material from the Leadville papers.

❧ THE QUEEN'S SUPPLIER

THE SPLASH MADE by Peter Holt in Laramie City's first frenzy of settlement was indeed small, but the legacy he left has made up for that.

Peter arrived in Laramie late in 1869 and so was counted with the 1870 Census. He was listed then as age 37, an age when vim and vinegar are most active.

Peter Holt opened a grocery store on Front Street one door north of the present-day Senior Center, and he advertised himself as Supplier to Her Majesty the Queen and to President Grant.

He sold the usual staples, fresh oysters, and fresh fruit in season—shipped daily via rail. He advertised salmon steak at thirty cents a pound, and whole salmon at twenty-five cents a pound. He soon bought the City Bakery and added daily fresh-baked goods to his shelves. He stocked housewares. Before long, fine confections and two soda fountains joined his choice offering. He was doing very well, and the Queen might have been pleased.

Peter bought ten acres a half-mile east of town and astounded the settlers by building a magnificent house. It stood in isolated splendor on the rolling plain and was called a "model of architecture," but was more often referred to as "Holt's Folly."

∞ *"Holt's Folly" the house Peter Holt built for his bride is still standing today.* (Beery Collection)

It was a study in Victorian design, later called American Gothic and Carpenter's Gothic, with articulately pitched roof, squeezed gables, ornate fretwork and welcoming veranda. This eye-catching legacy still stands, a monument to love.

For Peter was the hero of a romantic tale of lost love. It was said he built the splendid house to entice his love to Wyoming. She didn't come. It was said he was heartbroken, so bitterly disappointed in love that he never married.

Peter was disappointed in love all right, and he also had been married before his arrival in Laramie.

On January 3, 1866, at Steadmanville, Chataqua County, New York, Peter Holt and a lady with a name like a music-hall girl were married. By March 15, 1866, Floretta Castleman Holt was absent from the home of her bridegroom and never returned. The *Daily Sentinel* reported that Holt went east to try to get her to return, but she did not.

Why would a bride desert her home and ever-loving husband? Why did she not follow and share in the adventures and life of her mate? *Was* she a music-hall girl, reluctant to give up the glamour of stage-life for life in the unknown primitive west? Why could he not woo her back to him, even after he built his "Folly" expressly for her. Whatever became of her?

The years between her desertion and 1869 when Holt first appeared at Sherman, Dakota Territory, then Laramie City, remain a mystery. So does Floretta Castleman Holt.

Whatever reasons there were, their differences remained "unreconcilable." Peter sued for divorce from Floretta in July, 1871. By September he was a single man and Supplier to the Queen.

The next summer, the *Daily Sentinel* stirred a bit of interest with the item "Peter Holt is going East to get new goods we suppose, though it has been intimated to us that he is calculating to commit matrimony. Peter looked sort of guilty…and there is probably something to it."

If there was, it blew away. Peter returned alone and the subject was never again mentioned. Other things arose.

The Department of the Interior and the Union Pacific Railroad Company finally ironed out the problem of ownership of the Laramie town site, and, in 1875, the railroad company at last began to give clear title to town lots. They published a statement in the *Sentinel*: *"Parties occupying lots or who have built on unsold lots must either purchase them or vacate them without delay."*

Peter was among those who could not again buy the land they thought they owned and had improved. He lost the ten acres even though he held clear title to his Folly. The title did him no good, for that property was now heavily mortgaged and with business falling off, Peter had to let it go.

A bit sour on the world, the Queen's Supplier tried to hold off creditors who were pressing for payment. He sold five thousand dollars worth of produce raised on his 10-acre plot and that satisfied most of the creditors. He closed his store and opened a bar and rooming house at Cheap John's old stand near the corner of Second and C (Garfield), which he called the Centennial, and so returned to an earlier occupation, that of bartender. He mentioned the Queen no more.

With some twenty-five to thirty drinking places operating in town, business was not pressing any of them. Small debts continued to grow and nagged at Peter. He, being honorable, tried to keep up payments, but there was a limit. It was reached on the day John Davis, a creditor, called to ask for payment.

Peter had had enough. The added humiliation of being dunned *publicly* was too much. He picked up a big knife and went after Davis. Davis scrambled for the door. He suffered a few cuts, and the back of his coat caught most of the angry slashing. Holt was stopped when a customer forcibly applied a stove-poker to his head.

"Hated to do it," the customer admitted to the police. "But Pete was crazy drunk. He could of killed Davis."

So, in addition to Davis's bill, Peter had to pay court costs and the doctor bill for his own gashed head.

In ten years Holt had lost all his holdings, his bride, and the fine house he had expected her to grace, his grocery-bakery business, and the final blow—the saloon which had been a last resort. Peter gave up.

The Queen and President Grant lost their supplier, but the 1880 Census shows that America's counterpart to France's Foreign Legion, the U.S. Army at Fort Sanders, gained one private named Peter Holt, age 39.

This may show how slowly time passes, or else Peter lost several years' growth to that stove poker.

∞

BIBLIOGRAPHICAL ESSAY. In 1947 Ellen Blake Fox gave a talk to a gathering on her memories of early years of Laramie. She stated that when she "arrived in Laramie City, in 1872 Peter Holt's elegant house stood out on the prairie east of town." This gives an approximate building date for that house which stood in splendid isolation for many years waiting for the town to reach it.

County records call it "Holt's Folly." County records also show Holt's ownership of various properties and dates of their loss to mortgage default. His newspaper ads and news items provide other details as well as the notice of divorce.

Census Records for 1870 and 1880 support the reports of Holt's age.

෧෨ ෧෨ ෧෨ ෧෨ ෧෨ ෧෨ ෧෨ ෧෨ ෧෨ ෧෨ ෧෨ ෧෨ ෧෨ ෧෨ ෧෨

An item in the *Laramie Daily Sentinel*, of July 19, 1890, reported:

A strange legend told by the Sioux warriors after the Custer Battle, says the *Denver Republican* newspaper, relates that a deadly plant sprang up on the hillock where Custer died. The plant, never before seen in this area, is tall with long slender leaves curved in the exact form of a sabre with edges so sharp as to inflict keen wounds on unwary hands. When picked up it feels strangely cold and clammy.

It bears a golden head with heart-shaped blossoms, and in the center of each is a small spot of brilliant red, like a drop of blood.

The Indians, says the newspaper, regard the plant with awe and superstition. They call it "Custer's Heart," and avoid it carefully, for if the blossom is crushed in the hand it leaves a blood-red stain impossible to remove.

෧෨ ෧෨ ෧෨ ෧෨ ෧෨ ෧෨ ෧෨ ෧෨ ෧෨ ෧෨ ෧෨ ෧෨ ෧෨ ෧෨ ෧෨

✠ FIGHTIN' PREACHER

ONTO THE WILD, free-wheeling scene that was Laramie City in 1875 strode a new, controversial character, a pulpit-pounding, shouting preacher from the hills of Tennessee, the Reverend J. A. Edmondson, pastor of the Methodist Episcopal Church.

Edmondson grew up in the Nashville area. His family were slave-holders, and he was taught to believe that slave-holding was a divine institution. Both interest and education seemed to uphold that idea, but on several occasions his faith in the philosophy of owning slaves was strongly shaken, and at last overcome.

One incident occurred while he still attended high school. Young Edmondson had stayed after school for help with a Latin lesson. A young teenaged mulatto boy rushed into the schoolroom, grabbed both Edmondson and the male teacher, and screamed for help and protection. Edmondson, then eighteen, and the teacher went to the door to see what was going on and were met there by two savage bloodhounds, followed by a man who was the owner of the both the dogs and the boy.

The slave-owner dragged the boy outside and sicced the dogs onto him, and while Edmondson and the schoolmaster watched in horror, the dogs tore the boy to pieces. Sickened by this sight, the young man questioned the divinity of slavery from that point on. But he realized that this was a demonstration of the cruelty of only one man, that there were other owners who treated their slaves humanely.

Young Edmondson completed his schooling and entered the ministry. He was given a pastorate in Alabama shortly before the beginning of the War Between the States. There was much discussion about secession and dissolution of the Union and whenever that subject came up, Edmondson bluntly stated his views.

He created a furor in his parish when he stated: "It would be a lesser calamity to abolish slavery than to destroy the Union."

This remark enraged a leading member of his flock who loudly declared he "would never pay another cent to maintain a man with such principles."

When war broke out, Edmondson enlisted and was appointed Chaplain of the Twentieth Regiment of Tennessee State Troops. They were enlisted under the Crittenden Compromise, a project whereby border states were to preserve armed neutrality. However, they were soon turned over to the confederates and joined heartily in the rebellion.

Young Edmondson then resigned and returned to Nashville where he spent the remaining months of the war caring for his parents. After their demise, Edmondson was appointed Superintendent of Public Instruction for Williamson County, Tennessee, under the half-military/half-Republican rule which followed the war.

As superintendent, he received government aid and funds from the freedman's bureau and a number of charitable individuals. He built school houses, hired teachers and bought books for the education of blacks.

"For they must learn to be independent and make their own way," he advocated.

∾ *The First Methodist Episcopal Church where the "Fightin' Preacher" was pastor never had bells.* (Beery Collection)

The Ku Klux Klan had other ideas, and he and they clashed. He met with much persecution and life-threats during the years following the war. His political views were as strongly expressed as his religious ones and with no less hesitation. He was soon reassigned to Laramie, Wyoming.

As a liberal southerner assigned to a northern pastorate, it would seem he might find kindred souls among his acquaintances in Laramie City. Not so. Laramie was just as biased as anywhere else in the nation, and the Civil War was fought over and over for years to come.

It wasn't long then before Edmondson's sermonizing brought criticism from aggrieved brethren in his church and in town. One of the most caustic and vocal was Methodist church member Charles W. Bramel, a Missourian. He was soon joined by N. L. Andrews, a Pennsylvanian, another member of that church.

Edmondson expressed himself emphatically on politics and religion alike and trod on the toes of high and low without mercy.

J.W. Connor invited him twice to preach in his saloon, the Wyoming Billiard Hall, and he accepted. What effect his preaching had was never mentioned, but Connor and another saloonkeeper shooed their bar-flies out every Sunday and escorted them to the Methodist Church. Special seating was reserved for the men, and they joined in the service with as much gusto as the regular members.

Edmondson's work aroused rancor, of course. In March 1876, C.W. Bramel began publishing a newspaper which he called the *Daily Chronicle,* often referred to by other editors as the *Kronk.* It was hinted that Bramel started the paper to hit back at *Sentinel* Editor J.H. Hayford, and now he added the Methodist minister as a target.

Bramel disagreed with Edmondson's political views and Biblical interpretations and publicly re-preached the pastor's sermons, adding his own interpretations. He took advantage of the announcement of the Sunday sermon-text published in the Saturday *Sentinel* and apparently worked up his own "sermon" for the day. He evidently made remarks during the sermon the next day, and he and his pastor crossed swords frequently. Bramel published his barbed criticisms in the *Daily Chronicle.* This led to confrontations with Edmondson and others who disagreed with him. Bramel and Edmondson often argued both religion and politics, and when they met one winter day in the street, Bramel knocked Edmondson down in the snow and slush. He had the grace to feel some shame for his action but never apologized to the minister.

The *Sentinel* reported the incident and added, "…the *Chronicle,* for party and political effect, comes out and published a threat against a minister of the gospel in case he should say anything in his pulpit against drunkenness and Sabbath breaking and in favor of law and order. But the minister ventures...to preach a sermon on these very subjects...."

Hayford went on to report some of Bramel's tasteless remarks and Reed (Bramel's partner in the *Chronicle*) "...comes out with a column and a half of vile, low, scurrilous abuse of his pastor, a tirade which would be a disgrace to a barroom blackguard and which, if it had any influence at all, was directly calculated to disgrace the religion which Reed professes, and injure the church to which he belongs, and destroy the usefulness of the pastor who is his spiritual teacher."

Edmondson replied through the columns of the *Daily Sentinel*. The two waged a bitter war of words through the two newspapers. Then N.L. Andrews jumped into the arena, creating much ill-will where before there had seemed to be only a loud argument.

Andrews, known about town as a wag and practical joker, *may* have joined the fray as a joke—to add more spice to the public pie. It soon became acrimonious and personal, especially when Edmondson announced he would preach on "The Gambling Hells of Laramie and The Men Who Frequent Them."

This was already public knowledge, and it shouldn't have caused the to-do that it did. Maybe if Andrews and Bramel had left it alone—but they didn't.

Bramel remarked in his paper, "If these places are closed, our city officials could never be re-elected." Hayford replied that the officials were elected for better reasons than to be re-elected.

Whatever reply Edmondson made in rebuttal must have stirred the Andrew's ire. In a three-quarter column of the *Daily Sentinel*, signed "For Good" [Andrews never put his own name to his words although everyone seemed to know they were his], he remarked on the attributes of a preacher and said that "...Edmondson came to us a refugee from justice...men are not selected to take charge of important business interest upon the recommendation of a bold brow and glib tongue... certain principles are...imperative [and] nothing in it should deplete a minister's manliness...his *antecedents* must be made clear and fair." [A slur against Edmondson's family, as slave-holders.] Andrews wrote at length on the matter of religion and a church that "gets bitten by overlooking these principles." Then he loaded his gun: "Are not all ministers to be estimated just as all men are? You cannot transform a *born rascal* into an angel of light by any amount of professed conversion, nor is such a man a fit occupant of a pulpit just because he has a forehead of brass and a bewildering tongue...."

The next day Edmondson fired back his reply: "We wish to say to this community that we did not come into your midst a refugee from justice...we came as a minister of the Lord, Jesus Christ.... We have declared 'Thou shalt not commit adultery' and it may be that *For Good* may have heard this and was burdened with his own guilts that this production of his is an effort to ease his goading conscience and he would like to make some minister a scape-goat.... Individual responsibility cannot be escaped."

Much of the by-play between these feudists must have been verbal, for many inferences are made in the newspapers that do not seem to have substance. N.L. Andrews does make the remark that Edmondson is not "Rightly Dividing the Word of Truth" at the time he "bounced and undertook to *bluff* our fellow citizens Pease, Lockard and Dawson and hosts of others [referring to the leniency of the judges in deal-ing with saloonkeepers, gamblers and prostitutes, as well as those occupied with that pastime]...and circulating scandal about our streets calculated to and *intended* to injure and blacken the character of C.W. Bramel."

Andrews poses the question: "Is this the same Edmondson that was Chaplain of a certain Confederate Tennessee Regiment and prayed for the destruction of Federal Soldiers? ...Is this the same Edmondson that refused to pay a certain publishing house [he omitted the name, showing a black line] $100 because the debt was contracted under the Confederacy?

"...he says he didn't come to us a refugee from justice... saying he is not as other men are...and says 'We have declared Thou shalt not commit adultery.' We challenge all holy, self-righteous, hypocritical scandal-mongers to do their best to lay bare and disclose all that has been seen or heard of sins that have been committed under cover of night. Again 'individual responsibility cannot be escaped.' Who is responsible for the woman of known reputation going to the study of the minister...at the hour of 11 o'clock at night February 16 and April 25th and May [date unclear]. Who stands before this community a self-branded hypocrite, pretending a holy desire to save the souls of *idiots*."

Edmondson inserted a challenge in next day's paper for Andrews to *furnish proof* for his remarks or face off in a court of law. Andrews did neither. The matter was dropped. But the damage was done. Edmondson's effectiveness as a minister was tarnished and the matter faced heavy debate at the District Conference of the Methodist Episcopal Church of Northern Colorado the following August.

Even the fact that the lady may have legitimately sought counseling and was not able to go to the church at a reasonable evening hour, nor in daytime, because of public opinion, was not enough to overcome the suspicions aroused. The lady may have even been one that Andrews, in his capacity as judge, treated so leniently on prostitution charges.

In spite of a petition drawn up and signed by forty business men of Laramie, stating their belief in Edmondson's integrity and asking that he be returned to this charge, and after all arguments brought before it, the District Conference decided it best to remove the Reverend Edmondson from Laramie. He was assigned to the church at Central City, Colorado.

When in July 1878, news reached Laramie that Pastor Edmondson and Miss Mary Donavan of Ottawa, Illinois, were married, Editor Hayford made a special trip to Central City to satisfy his own curiosity.

He placed the Hayford stamp of approval on the match: "The bride is a refined young lady, about 30 years of age, and of just the right quality to tone down the rough edges and corners of the Reverend Edmondson."

∾

BIBLIOGRAPHICAL ESSAY. Sources for this tale are furnished by the *Daily Sentinel* of Laramie, dated from June 1875 through August 1878. Any references or quote from the *Chronicle* were taken from the *Sentinel*, for there seem to be no copies of the *Chronicle* available for those dates.

Much was printed in the *Sentinel* which has been omitted from this story. While pertinent, it seemed to convey personal opinions of Editor Hayford and was repetitious.

Other material came from records of the Methodist Episcopal Church.

✒ THE JAMES BROTHERS— WERE THEY IN WYOMING?

A CERTAIN DARK GLAMOUR surrounds an outlaw. The thrill of planning a crime, matching wits with the law, the chase, eluding capture—it all adds to the excitement. Even now it lingers; we enjoy the thrill of living dangerously in the safety of our living rooms before the television screen.

The game of masquerade increases the excitement. Novice outlaws sometimes imitated a well-known gang to complicate pursuit or to borrow a bit of glory. The Wild Bunch, the Dalton Gang and the James brothers were often impersonated.

Photography was still new during the heyday of the outlaw after the Civil War. Positive identifications were difficult because few photos of suspected criminals were available. During their most active years as outlaws, no positive likenesses of the James brothers were published.

Several Wyoming legends claim that Missouri's notorious James brothers, Frank and Jesse, lived and worked in Wyoming in 1878 and 1879. Frank, the elder, is said to have whooped it up in the Hole in the Wall country. Legend also says the pair "had a ranch" in the Little Goose Creek Valley where the village of Big Horn now stands.

Further accounts state that Fred W. Hesse found a tree branch which had "Jesse James 1879" carved on the underside.

185

Hesse found the branch near a barn on the 28 Ranch located about twenty miles south of Buffalo when he was butchering hogs under a tree. He sawed it off and kept it.

Agnes Wright Spring, historian, states in her book "That Frank James was with the road agents when the Cheyenne-Black Hills stagecoaches were stopped [in Wyoming] is probably true.... There is no positive proof, however, that Jesse James helped to rob those coaches though he was known to have been working with some of the men caught in connection with the stage robberies."

Another tale links Jesse and frontier lawman N.K. Boswell of Laramie. The account states, "Jesse was arrested and put in jail on one occasion by N.K. Boswell of Laramie." He reportedly escaped with the aid of Ruth Hadley Bramel, who was supposedly a cousin of Jesse's and was the wife of jailer Walter S. (Buck) Bramel. Other versions of the story have Jesse being released unrecognized, for want of evidence.

The *Cheyenne Sun* reported in October 1881 that one of the James brothers was pursued by "brave and skillful officers" but attempts to capture the outlaw failed.

The *Laramie Sentinel,* reported Jesse James's release from the Green River, Wyoming, jail in 1882. The *Casper Tribune* reported Jesse James in Wyoming is 1894.

With so many details of the activities of the James brothers in Wyoming, one might assume the stories have credibility. That assumption would almost certainly be incorrect.

✳

During the Civil War, Frank James rode with the guerrilla band of Quantrill beginning in 1862. Jesse later joined with Quantrill's Raiders as well.

After the war ended, the brothers formed their gang, and their first foray was on October 30, 1866, when they held up a bank in Richmond, Missouri.

Over the next ten years, they and their partners robbed five banks, four trains, three stagecoaches, and a savings and loan company. They operated mainly in Missouri and Arkansas, with occasional incidents in Iowa, Illinois and western Kentucky.

On September 7, 1876, the James brothers and their gang held up a bank in Northfield, Minnesota. The townsmen were waiting. Three gang members were killed; four were captured, including the three Younger brothers. Frank and Jesse James escaped, although they were wounded.

Their trail led westward into Dakota Territory. There it was lost. An article in *Western Frontier,* in 1982, reports that "a man named Hunt, editor of the *Sioux City* (South Dakota) *Democrat,* helped them escape down the Missouri River in a skiff." Law officers learned that the pair were back in their home territory by October 14. It is reasonable that they would seek friends and family who would hide and protect them.

William A. Settle, Jr. in his book *Jesse James Was His Name* writes, "...descriptions of participants in crimes who were believed to be Frank and Jesse had, through the years, been wildly inconsistent as to height, weight, shape of face, color of hair and whiskers. Until Jesse's death and Frank's surrender, both gunmen moved about in comparative freedom throughout Missouri and in other states."

Jesse was afflicted with granulated eyelids and was forced to blink his eyes rapidly. However this information was not widely reported, allowing lawmen in-the-know to more easily spot imposters. They didn't blink right.

There is some question of the whereabouts and activities of the James brothers in the months following the Minnesota scrape, but both men bore wounds which required treatment and time for healing. And Jesse had two old bullet wounds to the right lung, acquired years before, which still gave him trouble from time to time, requiring quiet and rest.

Settle says in his book that Jesse spent several months following the holdup in Callaway County, Missouri, with the Washington R. Tidwell and Allen Womack families.

For three years following the Northfield holdup the James brothers were comparatively quiet. Spottings of the brothers were made in Leadville and Chaffee, Colorado, where they were supposedly prospecting and gambling, as well as in many other places. This is the time period during which legend places them in Wyoming, holding up a stagecoach and carving on a tree.

Ted Yeatman of Tennessee relates that the pair were farming, under aliases, near Nashville. Jesse went as "Dave Howard" and Frank and Annie as "Ben J. and Fannie Woodson."

Yeatman relates, "Frank lived close to Nashville and Jesse some miles away near Waverly. Jesse's farm was in a marshy area known as 'Big Bottom', a breeding ground for malaria-bearing mosquitoes.

"Jesse contracted malaria and for most of 1878 was laid up, often unable to do even routine farm chores. Recurrent attacks of the fever plagued him for the rest of his life; much of the time when he was supposedly active in some distant endeavor, he was really laid up with malaria."

During their Tennessee years, all of the James children were born. Jesse and Zerelda's first child, Jesse Jr., was born August 30, 1875. In February 1878, their twin sons were born. They lived only a few months.

When Frank and Annie's son, Robert Franklin, was born February 6, 1878, and Annie could not nurse him, Zee did.

On July 17, 1879, Jesse and Zee had a daughter, Mary Susan. They were still living in Tennessee.

Both men were plainly devoted to their wives and children. It seems unlikely that Jesse would have been prowling the country, leaving his beloved Zee to mourn the loss of their twins alone. With babies arriving regularly, Jesse must not have strayed too far from home for any length of time.

Frank found he could do well at farming. Jesse did not. Between malarial bouts, he bought and sold livestock, often race horses. Jesse bet on horse races and gambled.

After this three year lull from outlaw activity, the lure of easy money again bit the brothers. When the brothers ran low on funds, they called on the Chicago and Alton Railroad on October 7, 1879, in Missouri. They committed five more robberies in 1880 and 1881. In November 1881, Jesse moved his family to St. Joseph, Missouri.

On April 3, 1882, Jesse was betrayed by a young member of his gang, Bob Ford. Ford shot Jesse in the back, killing him, when in was a guest in the James family dining room. After Jesse's death, Frank began making conciliatory overtures to law officers. He surrendered and was acquitted of the only crime he was charged with. He lived until 1915, never traveling west of the Missouri.

✳

So let's take a look at the stories of the James brothers in Wyoming.

It seems unlikely that the brothers had a ranch in the Little Goose Creek Valley in 1878. They had no reason to come west. They were able to live in Tennessee under aliases; both brothers had children born in early 1878; Jesse was often ill from malaria.

Fred W. Hesse, who found the tree branch carved with the name of Jesse James and the date 1879, most likely did find the branch. However, there is no proof that James himself carved the name.

As for being sighted robbing the Cheyenne-Deadwood Stage, one must ask, why would the James brothers come to Wyoming, unfamiliar territory, mingle with a strange gang, and operate here under their own names. Chances of big loot in this wilderness were not *that* good.

The stage was held up at eleven on the *night* of September 13, 1878. D. Boone May was riding shotgun. (He later turned to highway robbery himself.) May "recognized" Frank James as one of the road agents—a great example of night-vision, especially when May had never seen James before. He hadn't even seen a photograph of Frank.

As for the escape from the Laramie jail with the assistance of his cousin—not likely. True, both jailer Buck Bramel and his wife Ruth were from the James's home stomping grounds in Missouri. But Ruth was dying of consumption and often pregnant. It is unlikely Mrs. Bramel saw any of the prisoners or helped in escapes.

Further, a letter from Milton F. Perry, Superintendent of the "Friends of the James Farm" Museum at Kearney, Missouri, states the names of Hadley or Bramel do not appear in any of the James genealogies.

It is unlikely that the Cheyenne officers were in hot pursuit of Jesse James in October 1881. In late September 1881 Jesse was involved in a Missouri train robbery and in November 1881 he moved his family from Tennessee to St. Joseph, Missouri. Logistics make it improbable that he was in Cheyenne between those dates.

It is most unlikely that Jesse James was released from the Green River, Wyoming, jail in 1882 or that he was spotted in Casper in 1894. He died in Missouri in early April 1882.

Jesse died many times during his years of activities. The *Laramie Daily Sentinel* reported each capture, each shooting, and each death.

The name and fame of the man lived long after him. Perhaps the late-comers learned to "blink" right, or they may have cultivated the "James breath."

The *Liberty* (Missouri) *Tribune* was probably right to label all the far-flung James brother legends, and especially the Wyoming tales, as "Humbug Big!"

∞

BIBLIOGRAPHICAL ESSAY. The legend of the James ranch in the Little Goose Creek Valley and of the stagecoach robberies is recorded in the previously cited *Cheyenne-Black Hills Stage and Express Routes* by Agnes Wright Spring.

Fred Hesse's account of the tree branch is from the *Buffalo Bulletin* (Buffalo, Wyoming: July 2, 1959, Fair Issue). Special thanks to Patty Meyer, Historian at Johnson County Library, Buffalo, Wyoming.

Jesse James Was His Name by William A. Settle, Jr. (Lincoln: University of Nebraska, 1977) proved most helpful. The chronological order of the gang's activities requires careful reading and comparing. Otherwise, the book was an invaluable help.

Magazines consulted included the *Annals of Wyoming* (November 1924, April 1958, and April 1966); an article titled "Jesse and the Cloth" by Marijo Gibson in *The West* (June 1970); the article "Jesse James in Tennessee" by Ted P. Yeatman in *True West* (July 1985); an article, no author given, entitled "King of the Bandits" in *Western Frontier* (November 1982); and an article in *Wild West* (October 1988) titled "Raiders Repulsed By Fire."

A letter from Milton F. Perry, Superintendent of The Friends of the James Farm Museum, Kearney, Missouri, in 1979 stated that no Hadleys or Bramels could be found in the James family tree.

Ted P. Yeatman, Nashville, Tennessee, answered my questions regarding the Jameses in Tennessee in a letter of 1979.

The Laramie *Weekly Sentinel* issues of March 11, 1882; November 29, 1879; February 28, 1880; and November 5,

1881 were helpful. The Cheyenne *Sun*, October 29, 1881, reported the chase of a James brother in Cheyenne.

Another useful book is *Jesse James, My Father* by Jesse James, Jr. Young Jesse tells of his father's years immediately after the Civil War and touches briefly on his outlaw escapades. He states that Jesse had only two photographs taken during his lifetime, and they were always held by the family. Also, Jesse Jr. says many of the holdups attributed to the James brothers were none of their doing. He also states his father and uncle did not identify themselves during any of their outlawry, so those bandits who snarled "I am Jesse James", or "I am Frank James" were among the imitators. Jesse also puts the brothers in the southern states, except for the Minnesota foray.

An interesting book is *The Rise and Fall of Jesse James* by Robertus Love originally published by Putnam Brothers, New York, in 1926. Love knew Frank James and later met Jim Cummins, a member of the gang in a few of their escapades. Love's story distinguishes the hold-ups really made by the outlaw gang. His information comes from Frank James and never places the brothers west of Lawrence, Kansas. At the end of the book Love tells of Jim Cummins whom he became acquainted with after Jim's return from Wyoming.

Jim Cummins' Book Written by Himself, a True But Terrible Tale of Outlawry by Jim Cummins was published by Reed Publishing Company, Denver, Colorado, in 1903. In his "Terrible Tale" Cummins relates the various forays in which he took part with the James longriders. These were centered in Missouri and Arkansas. Cummins did not take part in the Northfield fiasco. He did not join the brothers in Tennessee. He didn't like Jesse nor Frank, so left their country. He says the James brothers and their toughs were never in Wyoming, except when Frank and another unnamed rider were in Cheyenne for two or three days.

Cummins himself lived in Buffalo, Wyoming, for some time operating a shoe store under the name of Johnson. He took part in town activities and lived a blameless life, making many friends, and no one believed him when he claimed to be *the* Jim Cummins of James gang fame.

The Missouri authorities wired to Buffalo that they had no reason to want Cummins. The response was the same from Arkansas. The claim "Johnson" made and the response it stirred up was echoed in Hayford's *Sentinel* of the period. Cummins had a tough time trying to convince any peace-keeping authority that he was an outlaw. He finally was forced to accept the fact that he was not notorious, not wanted by the law anywhere and was a free man, able to go wherever he liked.

He returned to his home territory and lived out his life there, puzzled but free.

~∞~ ~∞~ ~∞~ ~∞~ ~∞~ ~∞~ ~∞~ ~∞~ ~∞~ ~∞~ ~∞~ ~∞~ ~∞~ ~∞~ ~∞~

RULES OF THE TAVERN

LEGEND HAS IT THAT THESE RULES WERE POSTED IN MANY
FRONTIER TAVERNS, HALF IN JEST, HALF IN EARNEST

FOUR PENCE A NIGHT FOR A BED.
SIX PENCE FOR SUPPER.
NO MORE THAN FIVE TO SLEEP IN ONE BED.
NO BOOTS TO BE WORN IN BED.
NO BEER ALLOWED IN THE KITCHEN.
NO DOGS ALLOWED UPSTAIRS.
NO RAZOR GRINDERS OR TINKERS TAKEN IN.
ORGAN GRINDERS MUST SLEEP IN THE WASH HOUSE.

~∞~ ~∞~ ~∞~ ~∞~ ~∞~ ~∞~ ~∞~ ~∞~ ~∞~ ~∞~ ~∞~ ~∞~ ~∞~ ~∞~ ~∞~

❧ Dalton Gang

A DELIGHTFUL LEGEND persists that the notorious outlaw Dalton gang owned property in Laramie at 517 South Seventh Street.

A grandmother thrilled her family with the tale of the gang of horsemen riding into town one dark August night in 1905 to deliver the deed to the Seventh Street property to her and her husband.

Her tale has the men remaining outside, mounted on their horses and ordering the Hartley family to remain in the house. A member of the gang carried the deed back and forth for the proper signatures. When the transaction was completed, he and his henchmen rode away toward the eastern foothills and out of Wyoming. The seller of this house, she told her family, was Dalton, one of the famous outlaw gang.

Thrilling. Most interesting. But untrue.

In the first place property transfers were not carried out in this fashion, not even back in the days of 1905.

In the second place, the Daltons of the real estate records are not the gang members. Alvin M. Dalton, who once owned the property, was an only son, and according to his wife Lenna, they were "not involved with the Daltons of infamous name, and [she was] tired of answering questions about any connection." And Alvin's cousin, Carter Terrance

(C.T.) Dalton, who was also the owner of the property at one time, was not related to the gang either.

Alvin Dalton owed cousin C.T. a sum of money, and to pay off the debt, Alvin signed the Laramie property over to C.T. Later C.T. Dalton sold to the Hartley family on August 1, 1905. He arrived in Laramie by iron horse (not the four-footed variety) and the transfer was made according to law in daylight. C.T. Dalton was an attorney and lived in Washington, D.C., at that time.

By 1905 the infamous Dalton boys had been mouldering in their graves in Kansas for thirteen years, so could hardly have made the trip to Laramie, either by horse or train.

✖

There were five famous Dalton brothers. In 1887, Frank was a U.S. Marshal. Robert, Gratton and Emmett were Deputy U.S. Marshals. Bill had gone to California and was a respected businessman, married, and campaigning for political office.

But that all changed when Frank was killed in the line of duty by whiskey smugglers in 1887. The three remaining lawman brothers soured on law enforcement and turned in their badges. They headed for California to visit Bill. They liked it on the coast and for two years they did well on the straight and narrow path. Then they heard of a train said to be carrying a treasure-trove of money. The temptation was too great. They held up the train, were identified and after a harrowing time made their escape and hurried home to Oklahoma and its safe hills. It was the beginning of their ride on the owl-hoot trail.

The publicity from the California train robbery ruined Bill Dalton's life, although he was not involved. He returned to Oklahoma and family, and shortly afterward, he, too, became an outlaw. "Got the name; may as well have the game."

∞ *Mrs. Hartley entertained her granddaughter, Florence Ware, with tales of the Dalton gang.* (Beery Collection)

Many robberies followed. On October 5, 1892, the Dalton gang attempted to hold up two banks in Coffeyville, Kansas, at the same time. Three of the brothers, Robert, Gratton and Emmett, were involved with others of the gang unrelated to them. Bob and Grat were killed at the scene, and Emmett was wounded. He was captured, nursed to health and sent to prison.

Bill was not at the Coffeyville bank robbery, but he was killed by a posse in 1894 at the age of 31. Emmett served fifteen years for the Coffeyville caper, was pardoned in 1907, went to California, was married, wrote a movie script about the Dalton escapades, and died in 1937 at the age of sixty-six.

Yes, it seems unlikely that the Dalton Gang was selling property on a dark night in Laramie in 1905.

❋

Another tale making the rounds in Wyoming history is of a man with a broken leg, taken to a Dr. Huson for treatment. Huson had a ranch on Crazy Woman Creek along the old Bozeman Trail between 1884 and 1888.

Huson set the broken leg and nursed the man back to health. When the man was ready to leave, he told the Huson children he was "Bob Dalton, just a plumb no-good train robber and outlaw."

He had reason to regret his wild ways, he told the children, for he held up a stage in which his mother was riding, coming to find her son, because "she couldn't stand him never writing to her."

Since he was masked, she didn't know the bandit was her son. His conscience troubled him sorely.

Since the Daltons organized and began their banditry in 1889, *this* Dalton could not have been a member of that group. And the Dalton name was not famous at the time, either. Nor did gang members act individually after they were organized.

The mother of the infamous Dalton Gang wouldn't have found the time to seek a wayward son who never wrote. There were fifteen Dalton children. One boy, Littleton, died in childhood. At the time of this story of Bob Dalton and Doc Huson, six or seven of the younger children would have still lived at home. Mrs. Dalton had many things to do besides traipse through Wyoming looking for a son.

Mrs. Dalton divorced her husband, Louis, and in 1889 moved onto a school quarter near Kingfisher, Oklahoma.

❋

In spite of all the proof to the contrary, many will continue to believe that the Dalton Gang owned the wee brick house in Laramie.

Well, it does make a good story!

∞

BIBLIOGRAPHICAL ESSAY. My research took me into the background of Alvin M. and C.T. Dalton. As a result of my query to the County Clerk of Burnet County, Texas, where Alvin M. and Lenna had signed over the Laramie property to C.T. Dalton, I received letters in 1979 from the County Clerk of Tom Green County, Texas, and from the John F. Dalton who had lived in Laramie from 1923 to 1944. Also, I received a booklet listing members of the Dalton family tree.

John Dalton later sent a copy of a letter written by Lenna Dalton wherein she states that Alvin, her husband, was an only child, that she was a sick old woman and tired of answering question about the Daltons, and her husband was not related to the gang. John F. Dalton is now deceased.

My letter to Coffeyville, Kansas, brought the newspaper write-up on the attempted hold-up of the two banks, the result, and a lurid history of the members of the gang.

An interview with Janice Lippold of Laramie provided information. She grew up on her family's homestead near Kingfisher, Oklahoma, and was a close neighbor to Adeline Younger-Dalton, an exceptionally kind and worthy lady. Janice Lippold is now deceased.

The house referred to as "gang-owned" is the one mentioned in another chapter in this book, "The Gypsy's Warning," built for Harriet Adelia Rice-Richards and H.H. Richards.

Other records concerning ownership of the building were obtained at the Albany County Courthouse and from the *Laramie Daily Sentinel* and *Laramie Boomerang* newspapers pertaining to that period.

The "legend" comes from unpublished papers compiled by Clarice Whittenberg, now found in the American Heritage Center at the University of Wyoming.

❧ THE TRUTH ABOUT SUSIE PARKER

S USIE PARKER, THE handsome black madam of early day
Front Street in Laramie, didn't rate much attention until
she petitioned the City Council to "allow re-opening of
her house." The petition, while favored by many councilmen,
was turned down. No reason was stated, which arouses
curiosity and much speculation.

The dusky maiden, as the newspapers referred to her, was
allowed to operate with few restrictions from 1894 until 1909
so long as she paid her fines as keeper of a house of ill-repute.

She operated as Sadie Parker and Stella Parker before
becoming Susie. This seems not unusual. The "girls of the
line" didn't use their true names, nor did they always give the
same name when appearing in court.

Or it may be that the justice misspelled a name or spelled
it phonetically. He may not have had the keenest hearing.

Moreover, as long as she *rented* her place of business
there is no mention of her color in the newspapers nor in the
city court records. Nor does there appear to be any difference
between the amount of her "contribution to the city" and that
of any other madam—until she bought property.

Even when she didn't pay her usual fine, the mayor kindly
excused her on promise to pay later rather than force her to
lay it out in jail at a dollar a day.

Things changed, though, in 1909 when she bought the Front Street property consisting of four houses facing First Street and a house and shed facing on Kearney. She lived in the Kearney house.

Ownership evidently made the place noisier. A week after the purchase, Harry Cummings plowed into the mayor's office complaining of the "existence of a so-called negro dive" in his neighborhood.

Mayor James Stirling told him the city had nothing to do with it, that he should make his complaint to the Justice of the Police Court. It got into the papers.

The *Laramie Boomerang* sputtered: "If the City has nothing to do with it, then why do they go down there and collect fines?

"Susie Parker is paying fines under which (city) rule permits her to operate her place of prostitution in a joint on First Street, and she may even display a large red electric light."

Knowing the question would arise, the newspaper stated, "The other two houses are not in residential districts so cannot be considered in the same light."

Citizens ranted because the mayor had not personally accepted the complaint, but Mayor Stirling had learned his lesson from an expert.

Back in 1903, James Stirling, as city marshal, had brought Susie Parker to court on charges of prostitution along with the usual clutch of madams. Susie had pleaded guilty. In answer to a question she said she was renting her place from Manasse through Rental Agent Crumrine. Susie was fined forty dollars, and as no city officials were present to take custody of her, she was discharged.

The judge had requested that Stirling have City Attorney C.P. Arnold present at the hearing. Arnold refused to come, pleading other cases.

Stirling was then told to file complaint against Agent Crumrine for renting a house for fornication. Marshal Stirling informed the court that "the City Council had instructed him not to enforce that ordinance or make complaint against any person or agent for renting a house for use as a house of prostitution," and that City Attorney Arnold did not think that any of the laws should be enforced where they relate to prostitution.

Stirling and Arnold were ordered to appear in court the following week, but Arnold again did not show and Marshal Stirling repeated the attorney's instructions. Judge Grant declared them both in contempt of court.

The see-saw continued. The keepers were brought in, fined and dismissed. Arnold and Stirling did not appear at the hearings.

By March, the angry judge was trying the keepers on vagrancy charges. Attorney C.P. Arnold declared the laws of the city ordinance were not consistent with the laws of the state. He cited six different crimes or lines of conduct, any one of which constitutes vagrancy and stated that the council clearly exceeded and violated the statutes of the state.

So Susie continued her business quietly until the matter of her ownership brought all the noise and frolics to public attention. And the red light was a sore spot, too, until an irate neighbor shot it to pieces. Then Susie was apparently told she could be assured of "protection" and privacy if she would build a high board fence around her place. She did. It shut out the sight of sinning but not the sounds.

Another thing that heightened the dudgeon was the question of who had told her she would be safe behind the fence.

The rumor was noised about that the City Council and Republican Party had given the dusky maiden this assurance because she "could deliver a big block of votes to the Republican ticket."

The majority of the Council at that time were what J.H. Triggs, in his 1875 City Directory, had happily termed "unterrified Democrats." So that bucket could hardly hold the worms.

With a minimal number of blacks in town, how much influence could Susie have at a time when women were an unconsidered factor in politics?

At any rate, Susie Parker continued to operate her resort—in low key—throughout the summer and fall, appearing regularly with other keepers and paying her fines.

Those fines were frequently less than the other madams', probably because each keeper paid her operating fee plus an additional amount for each boarder she "managed."

In January 1905, George Gerber was struck in the head and killed in Susie's house by William (Dicey) Burney, a person so light in color that he could, and often did, pass for white, and his buddy Henry E. Clay. They were convicted of manslaughter and sentenced to the penitentiary. Burney died in jail in 1906. Clay had been sentenced to hang, but was given a new trial since "evidence against him was polluted." Each had accused the other of the killing. Clay was sentenced to twenty-one years.

As a result of this publicity, Susie apparently did not operate for the rest of 1905 and all of 1906. By the following spring she was back in the public eye, paying her fines along with the other keepers. And when, in September 1909, Susie bought the quarter-block on First Street where she had run her business for so long, the real fireworks began.

The ownership, the red light and the board fence ruffled the town's feathers. Susie was arrested and put in jail along with her two companions.

The *Boomerang* of November 4, 1909, related that the three dusky maidens "will be tried before Squire Carlin at

Keystone on a charge of conducting a house of ill repute and practicing prostitution, and if they are convicted they will be sent to jail for six months and fined $100."

County Attorney S.W. Downey called Susie to his office and told her she must close up as a public resort. He stated he "didn't want to be unjust or harsh," owing to the fact that she had so long been permitted to run the place.

She hired Judge M.C. Brown as her attorney.

"Susie's house was dark last night," the *Boomerang* reported, "but some men were seen going in the back way." (The two inmates arrested with Susie had been released upon payment of their fines, so were still at the house. Susie was still held.) "And today," the newspaper went on, "one man went to the door in broad daylight and was admitted. Neighbors are watching closely and county officers are also alert. She cannot run her place, even clandestinely, without being caught, and if caught will be arrested again and again...."

Two weeks later Susie and her girls were tried in the court of Justice Victor Carlin at Holmes. They each paid twenty-five dollars. Susie agreed, through her attorney, to close her dive and keep it closed.

Rumors sprang up that Susie had bought a building in the 300 block on First Street near the other red-light places and would move her joint up there and continue to run it. It was said that the deal was made with Minnie Ford, the madam of one of the white joints.

This was only a rumor. Minnie did not own the property. Susie stayed at the corner of First and Kearney.

On December 1, the *Boomerang* roared: "Susie Parker has not missed a day or night running her disreputable joint since the recent lawsuit. She has kept the dusky maidens in stock the same as before and lately brought in another one. Justice Carlin's handling of these people is a mockery of the law. Shame upon shame! They think they can do as they please by paying a fine."

The *Boomerang* berated the *Republican* for saying that Miss Parker's place was "closed and had been" and "the Marshal says it is closed," and vowed that the "Republican administration has decided to let its pet run that alleged bad place without inconveniencing her to the extent of paying a fine.

"We can produce evidence that she is running. Men have gone there at night and been admitted and even in the daytime! Day before yesterday men went there as early as 9 A.M. and stayed until 11 A.M."

Probably they were discussing politics.

A week later there was another blast in the newspapers: "Two bawdy houses face prosecution. Judge M.C. Brown, attorney for Susie Parker in her troubles, late this afternoon filed papers before the County Attorney charging Minnie Ford and Mary Day with...running houses of ill fame. The two girls are conducting two such houses on First Street between Grand Avenue and Garfield.

"These cases evidently result from the closing of the Parker resort. Judge Brown said if Susie was closed the others had to go too and he now follows this policy of retaliation."

All was quiet then until January 4. Then it was reported that "Susie and her attorney can't use the Court for spite work. Susie must put up bond before a warrant is issued for the arrest of Minnie Ford and Mary Day who are conducting houses of prostitution in a completely segregated district in town where no citizen complains."

The City Directory for that period gives Susie's addresses as 603 First and 110 Kearney. She lived at the Kearney address.

Late in March, Susie's house was raided. The sheriff and his deputies "arrested Susie and six colored prostitutes and three white men, all having a most disreputable time." The nine were lodged in the county jail. One of the women pleaded illness, paid a six-dollar fine and was released.

Susie and her companions pleaded not guilty and were placed under bond. Susie's was set at four hundred dollars, the others at two hundred dollars each. The three white men were fined twenty dollars plus costs. All "were foreigners" (fortunately) so were released.

The newspaper informed "...this place has been running full blast under the protection of City authorities. Protests do no good."

No mention of the Ford and Day establishments or the West Side house, which also operated under protection of authorities, was made. Nor was made any mention that this protection had begun in 1868 when Laramie City first appeared on the map.

Susie and her girls were held in the county jail, first because of lack of bond money, then because of a full slate of court cases.

By April Fool's Day, Judge Carpenter denied Susie's appeal for release by habeas corpus and stated she "must stand trial on the merits of her case." Judge Stickney heard the case the next day.

Fine was set at fifty dollars, a six-month sentence was suspended and Susie promised to "be good or serve her time." Stickney "tried to smoke out who had promised the special privileges" if she built the fence, but the dusky lady did not say.

"It is evident," the *Boomerang* remarked, "that the fellow who made the promise...had her well posted...should the question be asked. This ends Susie Parker so far as the crime she has committed all these years is concerned...."

But in 1917 the lady was in court again, charged with keeping a house of ill fame and selling liquor without a license. Police Judge Salmons fined Susie and her two inmates eighteen dollars each. Susie pleaded guilty to the liquor charge and was fined fifty dollars and costs.

In June 1919, Susie sold all her property at First and Kearney to the Union Pacific Railroad Company.

Meanwhile, two blocks north in the other red-light district, the buildings occupying the 1868 site of the Mayflower Saloon and the site of Nellie Wright's Crystal Wine Parlors in the 1870s, had become the property of August Vogelsang. That property was rented by him to various ladies "leading a butterfly life." This was the property which, in 1911, Susie was rumored to have bought. But only after she sold the Kearney corner to the U.P. did she buy that desirable site.

In this building, the butterfly Susie opened a boarding house, and thereafter her doings excited little or no public interest. She died in 1922.

In 1924 the boarding house was burned. And in 1924 the Union Pacific Railroad completed their new passenger depot on the site of Susie's old resort.

And that is the truth about Susie Parker.

∽

BIBLIOGRAPHICAL ESSAY. All information regarding Susie is found in Laramie City Police Records, Albany County property records and District Court entries as well as Voters' Registration.

Newspaper quotes are taken from the *Daily* and *Weekly Sentinels* and the *Republican* papers of pertinent dates.

ℐ SOCIAL SCENE

U P TO THE TIME of her death in 1917, Jane Ivinson was the social arbiter of Laramie. Invitations to any kind of gathering at the Ivinson's sumptuous residence were eagerly accepted and cherished. Grocer Weightman was always assured of a sale when he mentioned that "Mrs. Ivinson is having steak (roast or prime rib) today." Her choice of viands was as readily copied by the town's homemakers as were Mrs. Astor's in New York.

So whenever "at homes" were observed in Laramie, those people in the higher social strata, or those who aspired to be, were careful to observe the finest dictates of etiquette. These rules as observed in Laramie were as rigid as those of the strictest in London society. *[See chapter titled "Martha and Mary"]*

The hours when guests would be formally received were printed on the hostess's calling cards. For more intimate friends, the hours might be handwritten. This was the "at home"—probably an assurance against drop-in company. Especially did the "society" of Laramie honor these special calling hours.

Most of the "name" families in Laramie had a hired girl, referred to as a maid. Or they might hire a "day" girl, one who worked on "at home" days or special occasions only.

The caller presented her (or his) card to the maid at the door. If, for some unexpected reason, the hostess could not receive guests, the maid would relay the message. The visitor would leave one of her cards, with a corner turned down to indicate that she had called in person. Etiquette also required that she leave two of her husband's calling cards. (Business cards were never used for social purposes.) Most ladies' cards were about two inches by three inches. Callers with the bluest blood chose the finest, whitest card-stock with their names tastefully engraved. Those of thinner blood were not so strict. Some lesser-bred citizens might use cards decorated with flower arrangements, landscapes, or birds with ribbons held in beaks. The caller's name might be printed on the flowing ribbon. However, this type of card was considered quite gauche.

The magazine *Victorian Homes* gives rules for presenting a calling card which were as strict as the card-stock itself. Etiquette required the visitor to hold the card case prominently in sight, (about breast high) in a gloved hand with the added grace of a lace-edged handkerchief as a background.

The style of case was as important as proper dress for the occasion. Especially stylish was a container decorated with petit-point. This added to the formality of the call.

A proper social call was short, about twenty minutes. Tea must be served and conversation must be light; no controversial topics were allowed.

If the caller was a gentleman, convention demanded that he hold his hat throughout the call. Both hands must remain on the hat brim except when he lifted the teacup. This signaled that his intentions were honorable. His call was limited to a quarter hour. No mention is made whether a longer call was proper if the friendship was of long duration or the gentleman caller was of a venerable age.

Visitors' cards were placed on a stand in the foyer or on a silver tray or plate on a hall table. Callers could then see who had preceded them and enjoy being included in the special social strata.

Visiting in Laramie now is more relaxed and decidedly less formal.

∞

BIBLIOGRAPHICAL ESSAY. The magazine *Victorian Homes* (1988) indulged in a lengthy outline for properly making formal calls, presenting a calling card, making special calls regarding births, deaths, parties, or newlyweds, and informing friends when a family would be out of town.

∽ ∽ ∽ ∽ ∽ ∽ ∽ ∽ ∽ ∽ ∽ ∽ ∽ ∽ ∽

IN 1882 JOHN BENTON MORROW LEFT MARYLAND TO
BECOME EDITOR OF THE *CHEYENNE EAGLE*. HE WROTE OF HIS
WYOMING EXPERIENCES YEARS LATER AFTER HIS RETURN TO
MARYLAND.

HE WROTE OF A PECULIARITY OF THE ATMOSPHERE THAT
CAUSES THE MOUNTAINS AND OBJECTS ON THE PLAINS TO
LOOM UP WITH ALMOST STARTLING DISTINCTNESS AT
TIMES...THE LIGHTNESS OF THE AIR PRODUCES AN ILLUSORY
OR MAGNIFYING EFFECT, MUCH LIKE A MIRAGE.

IN TALKING WITH AN IRISHMAN ON THE SUBJECT, MOR-
ROW REPEATS THE MAN'S STORY:

"OH, YES...'TIS A FACT NOW. ALL YOU'VE SAID IS
TRUE, AND MORE. WHY, WAN DAY MESELF AND A BOY
WERE ROUNDING UP SOME CATTLE. THERE WAS SNOW
ON THE GROUND. AND LOOKING AROUND WE SAW
ON A HILL A WAY OFF WHAT WE TOOK TO BE A BUNCH
OF CATTLE. WHEN WE WENT THERE TO ROUND THEM
UP WHAT DO YOU THINK WAS THERE?"

"I SUPPOSE THEY WERE HOGS OR SHEEP?"

"NO. THEY WERE ONLY *HORSE MANURE*."

"AND ANOTHER TIME," THE IRISHMAN WENT ON
WARMLY, "I WAS DRIVING ALONG WITH MY TEAM AND
I SAW STANDING ON THE ROAD WHAT I TOOK TO BE
A MAN WITH A GUN. THINKS I TO MESELF, NOW
WHAT MIGHT A MAN BE DOING WAY OUT HERE
TWENTY MILES FROM THE NEAREST RANCH. AND
WHEN I GOT CLOSER WHAT DID I SEE BUT A HAWK!"

"I KNEW THEN," WRITES MORROW, "THAT I COULDN'T
TEACH MY FRIEND ANYTHING ABOUT WYOMING MORE MAR-
VELOUS THAN HE ALREADY KNEW!"

∽ ∽ ∽ ∽ ∽ ∽ ∽ ∽ ∽ ∽ ∽ ∽ ∽ ∽ ∽

✌ THE POWELL CASES

I. FRED

LIKE ALL NEWLYWEDS, Mary Keane and Fred Powell expected to live happily ever after when they made their vows before Father Cummisky on December 23, 1882.

They settled into their home on Laramie's Lewis Street. Fred continued to work for the railroad and Mary, as did most women of that time, kept house.

Fred filed on homestead land on Horse Creek about twenty miles east of Laramie City and apparently planned to use railroad earnings to help make improvements on the little ranch. Powell divided his working time between the ranch and his regular job.

With a paying job, he would have had no need to take livestock not belonging to him, nor to kill cattle and sell the meat. Yet even before he and Mary moved to their ranch, he was taken to court to answer those charges. He was acquitted for lack of evidence.

In the spring of 1889, he was charged again; this time with stealing calves. He was released because the jury couldn't agree.

When Fred lost his right arm half way between elbow and wrist, he was forced to give up his job on the railroad, so he spent more time at the homestead.

Mary's father, John Keane, bought the Humboldt Hotel in the spring of 1890. He refurbished, redecorated and renamed the place the Gem City Hotel. The location on First Street was a good one.

Mary and Fred and small son Willie, five years old, operated the hotel for Papa John. The loss of his hand and forearm created a noticeable change in Fred's disposition and did not help the hotel business. After he became accustomed to the arm stub, Fred and Mary decided to move onto their land. By 1891, the homestead requirements were fulfilled and they had received their patent.

It was a shabby, not too well appointed place. There was little promise of much improvement for Fred found it almost impossible to work with one hand and a stub-arm. If he had an artificial hand, it is never mentioned.

Loss of his hand affected more than his working ability. By turns, Fred was pleasant, moody, morose and belligerent. His explosive temper hit family and neighbor alike. Even with the increasingly efficient help of wife Mary, there were many problems.

A tension also was growing in the community between homesteaders or small ranch people and the bigger, more affluent ranchers.

The location of Powell's ranch on lush creek bottom apparently aroused envy and resentment among some of the larger cattle ranchers. By 1891 most of the Horse Creek and Sybille area was under homestead, and this cut into the free range previously used by ranchmen.

Mysterious happenings began to occur with disturbing frequency shortly after Fred and Mary moved onto their claim. The big ranchers blamed Powell and other homesteaders.

Livestock disappeared, sometimes turning up on the wrong range. The Powells apparently made an effort to return

⚮ The Globe Hotel was known as the Gem City Hotel when John Keane owned it. (Albany County Historical Society)

strays as they advertised in area newspapers of stock "Taken Up" or "Estrayed onto My Property." Whether the strays were claimed by their owners in response to the ads is not known, but rumors of rustling seemed to increase. The homesteaders and small-ranchmen were suspected and publicly accused, Powell among them.

Beeves were butchered, the meat sold, brands cut from hides and disposed of. Any hide stretched over a fence or tacked to a barn-side to dry received close scrutiny. In some instances a hide with a legal brand prominently displayed hung on a fence or barn until it began to shrivel. This added to already aroused suspicions.

Powell was often accused. Court appearance and fines followed heel on heel. Powell's temper became more bitter and unreliable, so much so that Mary sued for and was granted divorce in 1892.

Her husband, she stated, had threatened her life with a loaded revolver when she was sick in bed, and another time he had chased her about the place with an open knife. Powell took their small son Willie and left, vowing never to return.

But he did. They patched things up and life continued as before.

Powell put a dam across Horse Creek creating a fine pond which he stocked with trout. He sold fresh fish and gave some away to friends. As a result he was obliged to post "No Trespassing" signs "especially for the purpose of those hunting or fishing."

In May, the annual school meeting erupted in violence.

Mary Powell, E.P. Baker and George Shanton were members of the school board. Mrs. Emma Day was the teacher and was pushing to be rehired.

Mary Powell had a letter of application from another teacher candidate to read to the board. Emma grabbed it from her. A tussle followed and the meeting broke up with no business transacted.

Emma swore out a warrant against Mary for assault. They appeared in Laramie court before Justice of the Peace J.H. Hayford. He said the problem was a neighborhood quarrel and should be treated as such. "You'll break the County if you keep this up," he declared and warned all Horse Creekers to cool off.

They didn't.

In August, Powell was accused of fence-cutting. He paid a fifty dollar fine. Buildings at the Oscar Rogers ranch burned. Buildings at the Thomas Birnie ranch burned. They lived in a tent until he could put up a new house.

A neighbor, Mr. Fay, charged Powell and his neighbor Mr. Morton with cutting his fences. E.P. Baker was running sheep in the Sybille and Horse Creek areas. He accused Powell of setting fire to the tent and herding outfit belonging to him. Powell denied the charge, stating, "...it was probably due to the herder having his campfire too close to the tent." Or it could have been live cinders blowing onto the tent.

Hayford released Powell.

Then Baker charged Powell with malicious trespass. Powell was found not guilty. Another charge of malicious trespass against Powell was heard by Judge Hance. Hance fined Fred fifty dollars.

A charge of cattle stealing brought a four month jail sentence to Powell. He served his time.

Meanwhile Baker lost a saddle. His fences were cut. Some of his horses died. He claimed they were poisoned. It was later determined they had died of pink eye instead of poison. (Pink eye is often fatal to horses.)

Cattle disappeared. Papa John Keane went bond for Powell when necessary until his own financial troubles caught up with him.

Five residents of the Horse Creek-Sybille area were charged with many of the infractions. A neighbor and friend of the Powells, William Lewis, was brought in on charges frequently.

In January 1894, Lewis sued the Swan Land and Cattle Company for malicious persecution. Swan charged Lewis with stealing a calf valued at six dollars.

Lewis's fences had been cut and his hay burned. He had received letters threatening his life "unless he mended his ways."

In August, Lewis was killed from ambush. Three bullets lodged in his body. The head shot was made at close range and apparently delivered when the killer thought the victim still lived.

The whole countryside was aroused, but there was no evidence to support charges against anyone. There was talk that Lewis was a rustler. There was talk that notorious hired gun Tom Horn had been paid to gun down Lewis. But Horn usually left a "calling card," a small stone placed under the victim's head, and no such calling card was found.

Powell stated that no hides were found on the Lewis property to support the rustling talk, not even *pieces* of hides were found. The Lewis ranch sold on September 2, 1895, without further ado. The killing of Lewis and acquisition of his ranch by a prominent rancher did not lessen the tension. It seemed to increase.

Powell showed friends threatening letters he had received. Like those sent to Lewis they told him to mend his ways. The third letter warned: "This is your third and last warning. There are three things for you to do—quit killing other people's cattle or get killed yourself or leave the country at once." The handwriting was poor in an attempt to disguise it.

He showed the letter to a friend and asked him to accompany him home for he feared for his life.

The reference to cattle stealing was mystifying also, for Powell had not disposed of any cattle for a long while.

Powell stayed away from the ranch for two weeks, but he had to finish his haying. He and hired man Andrew Ross went to the ranch to put up the last of the hay crop.

Powell directed Ross to go to the creek and cut some willow poles to repair the hay rack. As Ross was cutting the willows he heard a shot. It came from behind him and passed over his head. He looked around quickly and saw Powell fall, crying out "Oh my God!"

Ross ran to Powell's side and found him already dead. Ross mounted his horse and raced to the neighboring Fay ranch to report the murder.

The assassin was a crack marksman for one shot did the job. Examination of the grounds and surrounding area revealed a boot track, well sunken into the sand, indicating the shootist was a rather heavyset man wearing a boot about size eight.

The murderer had chosen his hiding place well, above and in front of Powell. After Ross left, the shootist had gone to where Powell had fallen, apparently prepared to fire more shots if he was not dead. But the shot went into Powell's heart, slanted downward and came out near the right hip.

The sheriff stated he had an idea who the man was that did the shooting, but there was no real evidence to back it up. It was rumored to be a Tom Horn job. It was also rumored that five other people in that section of the country were targeted and another killing could be expected within a few weeks.

Powell was buried in Laramie's Greenhill Cemetery.

11- MARY

WHEN MARY Keane met the young Virginian, Fred Powell, she fell headlong in love with him. Their married bliss apparently lasted until Fred lost his arm. His character gradually changed from pleasant and mannerly to selfish, self-centered and boorish.

Managing the Gem City Hotel for her father added nothing good to their married life. The hotel was never a money-making project. Even with the desirable location it was not prosperous. There were many hotels in town and most of them had "upstairs girls," a drawing card for much of the traveling public of the day.

Fred lost his railroad job with his arm; it seemed a good time to move out to their homestead. At least they could raise most of their food on a farm. Mary was positive all would work out well, and much of the time it did. Even with the tension building in the Horse Creek community, their personal life seemed to flow comfortably.

But accusations and lawsuits arose with increasing frequency. With each new problem, Fred's anger and bitterness grew, and he struck back at Mary.

There also were problems within the Keane family. Mary's mother died. Her father could not manage the Gem City Hotel, even with the help of sister Katie and her husband Joseph Becker. Becker had money problems. Keane lost everything he had and the hotel and all his property were sold to satisfy mortgages. Joe Becker died, and Katie seemed unable to face a life without him. Mary brought Katie to the ranch, hoping country life and a change of scene would help. It didn't; Katie died. And Mary's problems were compounded by the changing personality of Fred.

Fred and Mary continued to be plagued by charges of fence-cutting, burning of hay, stealing cattle and malicious trespass. They weren't the only ones. It seemed as if all homesteaders along the Sybille and Horse creeks had been sought out for some low form of harassment. The nerve-wracking tension increased, and Fred took out his anger and rebellion on Mary.

That was when Mary filed for divorce. Fred and Willie left, and then returned.

It may be that Fred found himself unable to cope with Willie who was still young and who was evidently quite spoiled. Or it may be he could find no way to make a living with only one good arm. Or it even could be that he realized he loved Mary and depended on her understanding and help.

He and Willie came back to the ranch, back to their home and Mary. And life on Horse Creek resumed.

Then Fred was killed. It might seem that Mary would have given up and moved into Laramie. She may have wanted to find the killer. She may have decided that no one was going to run her off her own property. Or four years of country life may have convinced her that *this* was her destiny. At any rate, she and Willie stayed.

She was now free of restraint. She owned their land with no encumbrances. They had acquired more than the original

∞ *Mary Keane Powell lived a long and active life, during which she was accused of many crimes and served time in jail. She outlived her husband and son, both of whom died violent deaths. She is shown here in 1917.* (Wyoming State Museum)

homestead, and living on the farm was more promising than a menial livelihood in town. Willie was a growing and willing worker.

The rough goings-on in the Horse Creek-Sybille area continued. Now many of the occurrences were directed at Mary and Will. The newspapers were full of news of harassment, and it may be assumed that much was not reported. Mary and Will were as determined as Fred had been, that no one would run them out of the country.

Mary was accused of robbery, arson, stealing cattle, burning neighbors' hay and stealing hay.

With the lush hay meadows the Powells owned, the charge of stealing hay seems ridiculous. Mary Powell was charged with stealing five-hundred pounds of hay valued at $1.50 and belonging to a neighboring English rancher, Sir Charles Kennedy. He took her to court.

Mary won that round.

According to Burns's account of the affair in the book *Pioneer Ranches of Albany County*, when the verdict of "not guilty" was read, one old-time rancher stood up and proclaimed, "This is a case of the Virgin beating the Lord. I guess I'll go and have a drink."

"Not long after that affair," Burns related, "Lord Charles lost a lot of hay to fire. It was thought to be in retaliation for prosecuting Mary. He decided he couldn't compete against the odds and in 1914 he sold out."

The odds Burns mentioned probably meant the friends of the Powells. There were always friendly witnesses when one of the Horse Creekers was taken to court.

At the time Kennedy made his charges in 1910, Mary blew up in a public place in town. Sheriff James Stirling was called and arrested her for "...loud and unnecessary talking, using threatening, abusive, profane and obscene language, and by rude behavior interrupting and disturbing the peace of the City of Laramie."

Justice Hugh Hynds found her guilty and sentenced her to thirty days in the county jail for her unladylike behavior.

That fall she was accused of setting fire to hay belonging to Mrs. Elizabeth Richardson. Value of the hay was set at $100, but bond was set at $2,500 and later reduced to $750. No reason was given for the reduction.

Mary was found guilty and again spent thirty days in the county jail and was charged four dollars in court costs. Mary must have uttered a number of unhappy truths in her "loud, abusive and profane" tirade, for no suit or accusation was entered against her for some time.

Apparently convinced that the lady could not be frightened off her farm, her harassment lightened.

Country life continued to be rough, but with Mary given respite, son Will was now promoted to the number one hot-seat.

III-WILL

Willie Powell was nine years old when his father, Fred, was killed.

Over the ensuing years, he heard the telling and re-telling of accusations and suspicions from Mary and the neighbors, and made numerous appearances in court with his mother. Will was no novice to trouble.

He was named with his mother in most of the charges and was invariably found innocent (especially as a juvenile). Willie's appearances in court with his mother, where he was never convicted of wrong-doing, may have given him some feeling of bravado and arrogance.

Operations at the Powell ranch were always small-time. The woman and boy did what they could, living part-time at the ranch with short periods of living in Laramie. Robert Burns states in his book that the place was never well-kept or prosperous. In 1908, Will Powell deeded two and a half sections of land to his mother. The deed was filed in January 1909. Mary already owned the half-section homestead.

Matters seemed to change for Will when in 1910 he was taken to court and charged with horse-stealing. Mother Mary was not involved. The charges stated Will and his friend William Frazee did "take, drive off, steal, carry away and drive away" twenty-two head of horses belonging to John Biddick, and all was done "unlawfully and feloniously." Will, now in his twenties, had to face the court as an adult.

Willie Powell wriggled out of the charges after a three-year litigation. He did spend some time in jail while bond was raised and the trial pending, but in the end went free. The reason: his sidekick Frazee had skipped the country while out on bond.

For a time, then, Will kept his nose clean, or if not, he wasn't caught in any mischief. He married, had two sons, Harry and Jed, was married a second time to a pretty lady with a young son, and seemed to settle down.

After repercussions from the horse-stealing charges faded away, Will apparently decided, along with a few dozen other people living in isolated areas, that the final passage of the prohibition law should not apply to him.

In the mid-twenties Powell was taken into court in Cheyenne and charged with illicit liquor dealing. He pleaded guilty and paid a fine, still getting off easy.

The thirties saw moonshining picking up. Numerous speak-easies flourished in Laramie, and many rumors told of 'shining out on Horse Creek. Revenuers dropped over that way now and again, but came away empty handed.

Then in March 1930, Sheriff E.A. Baily of Albany County investigated the Powell ranch. Will was arrested but released on a one thousand dollar bond, then acquitted, because the officers had searched without a proper warrant.

Baily, armed with proper authority and accompanied by Federal Prohibition agents, then made a raid on the ranch. No one seemed to stay there. T.J. Stromberg, a hired man, appeared to be living there off and on. Powell never showed up. There were no tracks, footprints, nor other evidence in the snow to show that the place was occupied. Powell was apparently spending his time in Laramie or in Cheyenne where his wife Billie Mae worked.

The searching revenuers found three moonshine stills on the ranch, "all apparently Powell's," but no moonshine was in evidence. The men tramped back and forth across the grounds, and at last one of them suggested they examine a wagon-load of manure standing in the yard.

They found, hidden beneath the manure and carefully covered, one hundred gallons of whiskey in eight ten-gallon and four five-gallon barrels. The liquor appeared to be a good grade. The officers figured it would probably bring $950 on the market.

The officers poured eighty-five gallons on the ground. They took fifteen gallons to Laramie and entered it as evidence. Also as evidence, the agents dismantled a complete distillery apparatus, practically new, with auxiliary equipment, and brought along a gallon and a half of whiskey from the cabin as evidence. The outfit had been recently cleaned and was disconnected. It was found in a well-built two-room dugout about a half mile from the Powell ranchhouse.

The sensational trial lasted about two weeks. The case was wiped from the dockets when the court upheld the defendant's claim that the state failed to show ownership of the still.

True, the still and liquor were found on Powell land, but no one had seen him living there recently, and he was never around when the officers showed up.

Powell was acquitted by directed verdict. Once again, not guilty.

Powell then petitioned the judge for an order instructing Sheriff Baily to return the distillery paraphernalia.

Powell then brought suit against T.J. Stromberg, the hired man, for stealing eighteen one hundred-pound sacks of sugar from the garage on the Powell ranch. Stromberg had testified against Powell in the moonshining trial, and it appears this suit was in retaliation for that testimony.

The Powells stated they had arrived at the ranch on August 20 around midnight and drove their car into the garage. They saw the Ford roadster drive by and identified the driver as Stromberg. They saw something piled in the rumble seat of the roadster. They heard Stromberg drive into the gate which they had shut and heard him swearing.

"We decided to follow him, but failed to catch him," Will Powell's older son Harry testified. "We did find seven sacks of sugar strung out along the road. Back at the garage, we found that eighteen sacks of sugar had been taken through a hole in the back of the building where a panel had been removed by a crowbar."

In the morning, Harry said he discovered Stromberg's car parked near the road. He examined it and found a pile of sugar on the cushion of the rear (rumble) seat, a flashlight on the front seat and Stromberg's cap lying on the running board.

Stromberg apparently tried to implicate the younger Powell son, Jed, testifying that Jed had told him his father owed him quite a sum of money, and if he didn't pay up soon, he would sue—or hijack the supply of sugar.

≫ *After a police raid at the Powell place a moonshine still was dismantled by authorities.* (American Heritage Center)

Jed Powell, closely examined by Lawyer Phelan, council for the defense, admitted he had told Stromberg his father owed him a considerable sum of money and that if he didn't pay him soon he would sue. But he denied the threat to steal the sugar.

Stromberg said he was in Laramie from six to eleven on the night of August 20. He stated he and Howard Collins went to the Pacific Fruit Express plant and spent the night in the bunkhouse there. Stromberg stated he had left the keys in his car and, when he went out in the morning, he found the car had been stolen.

Stromberg claimed Powell owed him wages for the weeks he had been working on the ranch, and the suit also covered wages allegedly due Archie Britain for ranch work. Powell and Stromberg "had words" over the wages on July 5, and Stromberg had quit.

Powell declared Stromberg's testimony in the booze trial had been in retaliation for their earlier argument over wages. And yes, Powell admitted, he did have sugar in the garage, one hundred sacks, stashed there to make whiskey, but he had changed his mind about that and just left the sugar in the garage. Will, his two sons and his mother were chief defense witnesses.

Stromberg's alibi of being at the Pacific Fruit Express bunkhouse was verified by Paul Collins, PFE iceman, who said he had gone into the bunkhouse for a pair of boots about one A.M. and saw Stromberg asleep in bed. Apparently, Stomberg's case was stronger and Will Powell lost the suit.

Earlier in that summer of 1930 Powell was involved in a hit-and-run case which occurred about nine P.M. on a Saturday night in July.

Killed was Jesus Elias, who worked with a section gang on the Union Pacific railroad. Elias, age 22, had been given a ride to town, was beaten and robbed of about thirty dollars and kicked out of the car at the Beagle Campground on North Third Street in Laramie.

At that time there was much bitterness between Mexicans and whites in the Laramie area. The fact that Elias was robbed by a white man apparently sent him into a rage, and he attacked the first Anglo he saw.

He picked up a fence post and went into the garage of the campground and went after the mechanic, L.J. Sherman. Sherman thought the man either drugged, drunk or demented. He threw him out of the garage and telephoned the police. Bernard Irene and Percy Epperson, night officers, answered the call. They arrested Elias.

As they were crossing the street to the police car, another vehicle came speeding along Third Street, struck Elias, and threw his body about fifteen feet, and sped away. Three tourists saw the incident and ran to the young man's aid. The officers asked them to take the victim to the hospital, and they set off after the speeding car.

The description and license number led them to identify the Chevy coupe as belonging to Will Powell.

Powell and his wife were registered at the Albany Hotel on Second Street. The landlady said they had checked in about eight P.M. They were noisy and apparently arguing. About 8:45 Powell left, came back once, but left again. He returned about 10:45.

The coupe had heavy dents on the left front fender, the headlight was broken out, windshield glass was shattered and lying on the floor of the car. Sherman reported that the car had gone up the street from the campground and made a sharp turn, running into the red mud at the side of the street.

The officers found red mud on the fenders, running board and tire of Powell's coupe.

Powell was arrested. He admitted the car was his, but claimed that he was not driving it at the time. He and his wife had just arrived from Denver; he had parked his car behind the Albany Hotel and registered for the night. He said the car must have been stolen.

Plausible enough. Cars were not locked and keys were frequently left in the ignition in those days. It was a temptation for youngsters to "swipe" a car and set off on a joy-ride. Supposedly, when the joy-riders saw what they had done they made a fast getaway, parked Powell's car and fled. They probably were too horrified and frightened to confess. They probably were greatly relieved when Powell was accused and more relieved when he was released. Will Powell was acquitted since no one had identified the driver.

By then Powell's two sons were grown and off on their own. Harry lived in Oklahoma and Jed in Laramie.

Billie Powell's son, Alonzo Phelps, apparently lived part of the time at the ranch. He was there during the Christmas vacation of 1934-35. Billie had returned to work in Cheyenne after the holidays. It is plain that fifteen-year-old Alonzo and his step-father didn't get along.

On the night of January 5, 1935, Will set up a bathtub for the boy and told him to take a bath. Alonzo said he didn't want a bath. Powell insisted, and Alonzo again refused, saying "...in fact, I know I'm not going to take that bath."

Powell shouted: "You're going to take that bath. I'm going to have you do something my way for once."

He struck the boy in the head with his fist, knocking him backward over a woodbox. Alonzo scrambled to his feet and ran into a bedroom with Powell after him.

The boy yelled at Will to leave him alone and grabbed a revolver, again warning Powell to keep away. Powell lunged, hit the lad again, knocking him across the bed, and then leaped upon him. Mary Powell heard the racket and came to the doorway just as Alonzo pulled the trigger. One shot went wild and struck Mary Powell's arm.

Alonzo fired three times. Will was struck at least once in the abdomen and slumped away from young Phelps.

The three immediately got into the truck and headed for Laramie. Powell declared he would drive, but after a few miles he was in such pain he turned the driving over to young Alonzo.

The country road in January was frozen and rutted, and the rough drive did Powell no good.

On the way to town, Will told his mother and the boy they must say the shooting was an accident.

They drove immediately to the hospital where doctors treated Mary's arm and began at once to operate on Will. He died of his wounds the next day.

The boy tried to tell the same story as Powell. But when

Billie Powell arrived from Cheyenne, she began to talk with her son and Mary Powell. She told the youth to tell the truth.

Welts on his back, his forehead and behind his ear were shown to officers and a physician who declared them less than twenty-four hours old. Some were still red and not yet black and blue.

Alonzo was charged with second-degree murder because the shooting was not premeditated. He was acquitted on a plea of self-defense.

Thus ended Will's checkered career. He, at last, had to face the consequences of some of his actions.

＊

Like the old fighter she was, Mary Keane Powell died with her shoes on. Her long life ended in 1941, a victim of a heart attack.

She was visiting her daughter-in-law Billie May Phelps Powell in Cheyenne when she was stricken. She lived eight days. She was eighty-two.

∞

BIBLIOGRAPHICAL ESSAY. Information for this chapter is all taken from the *Laramie Sentinel*, both daily and weekly, from the *Republican*, the combined *Republican-Boomerang* and the *Laramie Boomerang*, from Albany County Court records and from Wyoming State Archival records of the trials.

I have taken verbatim news reports to create the story and have also taken license in some instances suggesting a reason for certain actions.

LOUIS E. "B.S." THOMSON SAID THE SMITH-AND-NORTH CREEK WHICH RUNS INTO DOUGLAS CREEK IN THE SNOWY RANGE WAS NAMED FOR TWO PROSPECTORS WHO LIVED ON THE UPPER END OF THE CREEK. THEY SHARED A CABIN WHILE THEY WORKED THEIR CLAIMS. ONE WOULD COOK AND KEEP HOUSE ONE WEEK WHILE THE OTHER WORKED THE CLAIM. THE NEXT WEEK THEY SWITCHED.

CABIN FEVER SET IN. NORTH BEGAN TO COMPLAIN ABOUT THE WAY SMITH COOKED. SMITH COMPLAINED ABOUT THE WAY NORTH KEPT HOUSE. COMPLAINTS GREW TO A MILD QUARREL. SMITH TOLD HIS PARTNER HE COULD MOVE OUT AND LIVE AS DIRTY AS HE WANTED.

TOGETHER THEY BUILT A CABIN ON THE OTHER SIDE OF THE CREEK. NORTH MOVED OVER. SMITH WAS A SUPERIOR COOK OF SOUR-DOUGH BREADS AND PASTRIES, AND NORTH WAS ESPECIALLY GOOD AT COOKING MEAT AND WILD GAME. THEY SHARED THEIR MEALS, WORKED THE CLAIMS TOGETHER, YET LIVED APART.

WHEN THE CLAIMS BEGAN TO PLAY OUT, THEY CON-TRACTED TIMBER-CUTTING. WHEN THE LUMBER BUSINESS SLACKED OFF, THE TWO SEEM TO HAVE FADED INTO OBLIVION, LEAVING BEHIND THEIR MYTH AND THE CREEK.

❧ A MAN NAMED ROPER

ROPER'S ROW WAS built on a grassy slope rising above the Smith-and-North Creek in the Snowy Range Mountains. Billy Roper had landed there in the mid-1880s, one of his friends said, running from owners of a silver mine where he had been working.

"He had weak lungs, so he couldn't work down in the mine, but he could sort the ore. Like so many of the other sorters, he became a high-grader. It was fairly easy. These men worked nights, with little or no supervision, and they could set aside some of the high-grade silver ore and smuggle it out at the end of their shift. Mr. Roper hid his beneath the floor of his cabin. When he had a fair-size cache, he would haul it out and sell it. He was afraid the mine owners were on to him so decided to leave. He loaded his ore into his old wagon, piled his household goods on top and made ready to take out. It was spring and the ground was thawed and soggy. His team was weak from the cold winter, and they couldn't even budge that wagon going downhill. Mr. Roper picked out a few bits of high-grade, unhitched the horses and lit out, sure the mine owners were on his tail. He never went back.

"He rode one horse and used the other as a pack animal and took off across country. He went through rangeland and private graze, opened gates, jumped streams and threaded

∾ *William Roper stands on the balcony of his Roper's Row Lodge.* (Beery Collection)

through forests, and finally stopped in the Snowy Range here in Wyoming. He located gold here and put up his cabin and stayed."

Well, that's a good story, as Louis Earl Thomson told it, but Thomson was known to intimates as "B.S." Thomson just *because* he told a good story.

Yes, Billy Roper had worked in a silver mine in the mountains above Boulder and Nederland, Colorado. He might have been a high-grader, which, though illegal, wasn't considered a black crime, but he didn't need to. He owned a fair share in a mine called the Shiner, and in 1884 when he came to the Snowy Range, he came with his partners. They were attracted by wild rumors about the richness of the Rambler Copper Mine.

Roper's partners, Charles B. Ritchie, A.J. Overholt, George V. Clark and William Griffith, had located several

likely prospects along clear-flowing Douglas Creek and its
tributaries. Billy Roper and Will Griffith bought the sites from
their partners. The other men returned to Colorado, and the
two Bills began panning for gold in the Douglas Creek riffles.
This stream, as full-running at that time as a river, romped
past the site of Roper's camp and caught the flow from the
Smith-and-North Creek. The sands the partners worked ran
about $2.50 per cubic yard. Griffith finally left but Billy
stayed on. He enjoyed the outdoor work, the solitude and the
view of creeks and meadows spread before his cabin.

The Jackson Placer Mining Company agreed to pay Billy
a monthly fee for the use of water from the Smith-and-North
at their works. They built a flume to direct the water and put
up a fine set of buildings. But the Jackson grounds played out,
and they couldn't pay Roper.

He said, "My pork barrel is empty. My flour barrel is
empty, and you won't pay what you owe, so I hereby cancel
our agreement." And he tore down the flume and all the Jackson buildings and moved it all to his property. He saved every
scrap, even the nails which he straightened for re-use.

On the slope above the Smith-and-North, Billy Roper
built a new cabin, which he called the Boar's Nest, and two
guest cabins, a wood and tool shed, a barn, three privies and a
two-story lodge with six rooms. He used hand tools—axe,
saw and square. The entrances to Roper's mines were well
hidden—in the back room of the Boar's Nest, in the black-
smith shop and in the first barn.

The lodge served as gathering place for locals from the
mining towns of Holmes and Keystone and lodging for
ranchers who ran cattle on forest land in summer. Tourists
spent a night or sometimes several, as did hunters and fishermen. Many a tie hack stayed overnight on his way back to
camp from a Saturday night dance at Fox Park. Besides a

good bed and warm welcome at the lodge, there was the privilege of a game of cards, gabfests or good reading, along with comforting samples from Billy's jug. For Billy Roper was a moonshiner.

When the gold began to play out at his mines, Billy took to making moonshine which he sold for a dollar a gallon. He made some beer, but that had less appeal than his rye whiskey. He also made a fine fermenty of fruit (fresh or dried as it was handy) which was well received. This was known as Roper's Elixir.

On occasions when Billy made a trip to town with his one-horse Cheyenne cart for flour, sugar and other staples, he invested in some store-bought whiskey. This was kept for medicine and sometimes shared with friends. There were never any drinking sprees or "goings-on" at Roper's.

"I remember one time Mr. Roper brought back a ten-gallon keg of whiskey," B.S. Thomson related. He always referred respectfully to his friend as Mr. Roper. "It was a high-summer day and a long, dry trip from Laramie out to the Row. We got up to the Jelm Post Office, which at that time was located where you turn off to head up to Albany at the south end of Sheep Mountain. There were several fellows there shootin' the breeze so we stopped, too. The horse needed a good blow, anyway. We had tapped the keg a time or two on the way out from Laramie, and, of course, while we were at Jelm, we tapped the keg from time to time, and first thing you know it went dry. And there went Mr. Roper's winter medicine. He managed to get through that winter, though, with the help of friends.

"Well, Mr. Roper's buildings all ran in a line along that grassy slope above the Smith-and-North. He had a hand-dug well which only needed a hand pump, the water table was that high. He always raised a big garden and irrigated from a ditch

Bobbie Thomson and her husband cared for Roper in his later years and inherited Roper's Row. (Beery Collection)

he put in between the row of buildings and the privies, which were lower down the slope.

"Mr. Roper was a great one for gags. He wrote Latin phrases and other lines on the walls of the privies. He never would translate the Latin for Bobbie (Mrs. Thomson), but he told me one line said, 'Wipe, or you'll smell bad.' He penciled quotations from Shakespeare, whom he quoted a lot. One line he wrote was, 'For this relief, much thanks, though 'tis bitter cold.' These were some of the mild ones.

"Bobbie had a couple of friends who visited from time to time. Mr. Roper would sit out on the porch and clap his hands every time he saw one of them go into the little house. Bobbie asked why he embarrassed her friends so. He laughed and said he was thanking them for adding to the meadow.

"Mr. Roper had a horse and a couple of cows, sometimes he kept a pig. And there was a pet deer that grazed with the cows. It was tame enough that it ate from a person's hand. One day a forest ranger stopped by and when he saw that deer he upped his gun and shot it. Mr. Roper was beside himself. He stuck the gun under the ranger's nose and said he'd a mind to shoot him. The man left in a hurry. Mr. Roper had no love for rangers after that.

"He had a fine large library. The southwest room on the second floor of the lodge was his special room. He had an intimacy with Shakespeare. He had many rare books. Many were in Latin. He and Victor Carlin [pronounced Car-leen] who lived up the Douglas at Holmes, were great friends. Each winter they'd get together to read, talk, exchange ideas and philosophies. They didn't always agree and sometimes would get into a hot argument. Then the visitor would leave in a huff, and there was never a word between them until the next winter when the former host would call on the former guest. Then the same thing would happen again. This went on every winter that I knew him. It didn't affect their friendship one bit, though. I think they enjoyed the arguments."

Thomson and his wife Edith, known as Bobbie to every acquaintance, had lived and worked at Keystone for many years. They saw Roper's Row as a possible business venture and also noted that the aging Mr. Roper needed care.

The Thomsons and Roper set up a deal for a summer camp for young boys between ages ten and eighteen who had asthma or other breathing problems. John Wicklund, a partner

∽ *The friends of William Roper "buried him easy" as he had requested.* (Beery Collection)

at the Fox Park Lumber Mill, "dozed a good road to the Row and hauled in two or more skid shacks."

"We hauled them on wooden skis or skids. That's how they got the name," Wicklund said. "These were used for those summer kids. The camp lasted two or three summers. But the Thomsons stayed on, loving being at Roper's."

On New Year's Day 1932, Bobbie cooked up a big holiday feast and invited friends from Keystone, Holmes, Lake Creek, Fox Park and Albany. It was sub-zero weather with deep snow, but they had a good crowd and a rousing great time.

Billy Roper, then eighty-three, ate a fair-sized dinner. "He had a duodenal ulcer," Thomson said, "and had to watch how much he ate. He had a last sliver of pie and decided he'd had more than he should and would go home to his Nest and lie down for awhile. It wasn't far along the Row. I walked him home, stirred up the fire, helped him undress and get into bed and brought him a mug of Elixir."

Then Thomson hitched his team to the wagon-box sled, loaded up the visitors and took the Albany friends home. It was past one in the morning when he returned. Bobbie was still cleaning up when he came in. He asked about Mr. Roper.

"There's still smoke from the chimney so he must be all right," she told him, so he didn't go over to the Nest.

But in the morning he found Mr. Roper on the floor, dead, his book beside him and the mug near his outstretched hand. The fire was out and the house stone cold.

The friends returned to bury the pioneer philosopher. They built the casket of wood Roper had saved for the purpose.

"You got it too big, boys," Bert Wallis told them.

"Well, we don't want to squeeze him," was the reply.

In accordance with William Roper's wish, they dug his grave across the creek in the south meadow, in a soft spot, and "buried him easy" as he had requested.

*

Louis Earl and Bobbie Thomson inherited the mines, real property and personal effects, including the "fantastic" library, from Billy Roper. They operated the lodge as a summer resort for hunters and fishermen for a time after the boys' camp came to an end. They looked after the aged Victor Carlin until he died in 1934. They inherited everything Carlin had, including his library, which was a match for Roper's. They worked the gold mines, filed on other sites, and kept up the assessment work. Returns were small. They finally sold the holdings and moved to Colorado in late 1949.

B.S. was stubborn, as well as a big talker. Thomson lived in the Big Thompson Canyon. He was eighty-six in 1979 when a flash flood roared down the Big Thompson River creating havoc. When flood waters carried away his cabin, he remained inside on a mattress. The mattress floated, providing Billy Roper with breathing space just below the ceiling. He escaped, wet as a rat, but unhurt.

Bobbie Thomson died in Colorado. Mr. Thomson was eighty-seven, in a wheelchair, and quite deaf at the time of our interview in 1980.

∞

BIBLIOGRAPHICAL ESSAY. I conducted interviews with Genevieve Thompson, Geraldine Lessley, Irene White and Agnes Henberg of Laramie. All had lived in the Keystone area. None knew Roper personally but had heard stories of his life. Agnes Henberg's uncle, Hans Olson, drove the team and sled that hauled the casket to the grave in the meadow. A letter from Myrtle Sawyer whose husband, Archie Sawyer, knew Roper, provided additional information. Both Mr. and Mrs. Sawyer are now deceased. An interview at Jelm with John Wicklund, now deceased, was helpful.

Laramie Daily Boomerang issues from the years 1907 and 1932 were an additional source.

∞ ∞ ∞ ∞ ∞ ∞ ∞ ∞ ∞ ∞ ∞ ∞ ∞ ∞ ∞

JOHN BENTON MORROW, EDITOR OF THE *CHEYENNE EAGLE* WHO CAME TO WYOMING IN 1882 FROM MARYLAND, WROTE:

"...AT LARAMIE CITY, SITUATED IN THE MOUNTAINS FIFTY MILES WEST [OF CHEYENNE] A CITIZEN WAS BOASTING OF THE STRENGTH OF THE WIND THERE WHEN A CITIZEN OF CHEYENNE SAID: "IT DOESN'T BLOW LIKE IT DOES IN CHEYENNE. WHY I SAW AN EMPTY BARREL FLY UP AGAINST A WALL AND STAY THERE FOR FOUR DAYS!"

"THAT'S A LIE" ANOTHER MAN PUT IN. "IT ONLY STUCK THERE FOUR HOURS, FOR I WAS THERE!"

ANOTHER MAN, TELLING OF A STEEP RAILROAD GRADE WHERE THE HANDS ALWAYS HAD TO APPLY A POWERFUL BRAKE TO THE WHEELS WHEN GOING DOWN, FOUND THAT THE WIND WAS BLOWING SO STRONG AGAINST THEM ON ONE OCCASION THAT THE WHOLE TRAIN CREW HAD TO GET OUT AND PUSH THE TRAIN DOWN THE GRADE.

∞ ∞ ∞ ∞ ∞ ∞ ∞ ∞ ∞ ∞ ∞ ∞ ∞ ∞ ∞

❦ Lone Bandit

WHEN BILL CARLISLE was seventeen, he ran away from home for the last time. He joined a circus and headed west, determined to find his older brother who was working on a ranch somewhere in Wyoming.

Bill's father, who was unable to work for long periods of time due to Civil War injuries, had been left with five children under the age of eleven. Baby Bill was soon placed in a home that accepted half-orphans.

As he grew older the lonely little boy took every opportunity to run away—seeking a home and family. He was always found and returned to the orphanage.

When he was about nine, his father came for him. The two eldest children were on their own. With only one daughter and a son left at home, his father wanted Billy with them. He was soon put to work selling newspapers. The money he made was turned over to his father. He squeezed out enough pennies for himself to pay admission to vaudeville and stage shows. He loved the fantasy of the shows. His father did not approve and whipped the lad for attending. Bill continued to go whenever he could and took the expected whipping when he got home.

Like many children in the Pennsylvania town where the Carlisles lived, Bill was sent to the railroad yards to pick up coal for heating and cooking at home.

243

The coal-picking was a daring "catch-me-if-you-can" game with the railyard cops who were called "railroad bulls" by the ragged coal-pickers and hoboes alike. The kids had no idea the cops were protecting them from injury or death by the cars. It was a daring, dodging hide-and-seek to the youngsters.

Bill grew to hate the bulls, but he admired the hoboes and hung around their jungles to listen to their tales of riding the rods and taking "luxury" tours in empty box cars. He was thrilled by the mystique of the railroad and the far places the hoboes visited.

He continued to run away from home during those early years. Somehow he always was caught by the railroad bulls, carried to the nearest station and returned home. Perhaps the rhythmic click of iron wheels racing over rail-joints lulled him to sleep or inattention.

When he was seventeen, he ran away from home for the last time. He wound up in northern Montana and found work on a horse ranch.

His boss was a horse thief. He bought just enough horses to shield his illicit side-business and set his riders to trailing the herds north into Canada.

The Royal Canadian Mounted Police caught up with the drovers. Owing to Bill's youth and obvious ignorance of the type of operation the boss ran, the young man was not charged.

The Mounties kept him around for a time, and he learned much from them, including values far different from those of the horse rancher.

When he left the Mounties, Bill headed for Wyoming, again seeking his brother. He found work on a cattle ranch operated by a man called Hard Winter Davis. Then he learned that his brother was not far away, working on a sheep ranch south of Kaycee.

The Johnson County Range War which pitted cattlemen against settlers and sheepmen was not forgotten, although it was some years past. The hard feelings still simmered.

When Bill visited his brother and asked for work the boss agreed—until he learned that Bill was working for a cattleman. Then the deal was off.

Carlisle worked at cowboying for the next several years in Wyoming, Colorado, New Mexico, Texas and back in Colorado. Between jobs he "rode the grub-line" as did other cowboys waiting for seasonal work. Sometimes the rider was given odd jobs on a ranch in exchange for his keep.

But Bill didn't stay long at any one place. He may still have been looking for a home and family.

While in Denver looking for work, Bill saw a man with a glass candy-filled pistol. Just the thing, he thought, for a gift to send to his small niece back East. He asked the man where he could find a pistol like it.

"The *Denver Post* is giving them away," the man replied.

"Will you sell that one?" Bill asked.

"Sure."

"All I have is thirty-five cents," Bill told him. "Is that enough?"

"Sure. It's a deal."

The toy was painted black with a bit of gold trim and looked just like the real thing. And the candy was good.

Bill's intentions were good, too, but meanwhile he was hungry. He ate the candy, but he kept the pistol.

He was in Green River, Wyoming, on a blustery winter day in February 1916. He was down to one nickel in his pocket with no prospects for a job.

He was at the depot in the western town when a passenger train pulled into the station. Carlisle thought of riding the rods on the east-bound train, no matter how cold it was.

By chance, the train's dining car stopped directly in front of the shivering cowboy. He was cold and broke and hungry. And before him were warm, well-dressed passengers seated at tables loaded with food served on the railway company's fine china and sterling.

Carlisle was highly conscious of that last nickel in his pocket, and suddenly was aware of the black-painted toy pistol beside it.

He stood there watching the passengers. He was cold enough and hungry, and the passengers in the diner were warm and looked well-heeled.

He stepped into the vestibule of a chair car just as the train began to get under way.

He pressed the toy pistol against the porter's back and directed him to pass his cap "accepting donations" from the men passengers. The bandit's face was entirely hidden behind a big white kerchief.

"Leave the women and children alone," Bill told the porter.

He received $52.35 from his first hold-up.

He got away. He also earned a price on his head and faced a life-sentence in the penitentiary for robbing a train. While posses scoured the Wyoming countryside for him, Bill was in Denver, where he found a job. He also found he was again working for a crook, so he quit and headed back to Wyoming on the Union Pacific, this time as a paying passenger.

A few miles west of Cheyenne, he tried his luck again. From that trick he got $506.07. He could have left the country and made a fresh start as no one had seen his face. However two days later he pulled another train robbery. He relieved the men of their money between Medicine Bow and Hanna. This time his take was $378.50.

As the train slowly beat its way up the Percy Hill grade west of Hanna, Carlisle jumped to the ground. He fell and sprained his ankle, but managed to hobble away into the dark, windy, winter night. He lost the toy pistol, although he had used a real gun on those last two hold-ups.

Posses found it easy to track him the next day. Because of his large feet, he was referred to as "paddlefoot."

He hobbled across the rough country through the winter night, hiding in animal-warmed barns to snatch quick naps. He tramped from ranch to ranch, an "out of work cowhand" stopping at isolated ranches between Hanna and the looming Laramie Peak.

He always stashed his gun before approaching any ranch house so he didn't present a menacing appearance. He was a handsome man and possessed of good manners.

It is claimed that the "dangerous outlaw" walked into the telegraph office in Casper and sent a telegram of thanks to the Union Pacific officials the day after that holdup.

Traveling afoot ninety or so miles across Shirley Basin on a dark night in deep winter is quite a feat even for someone without a sprained ankle, so that legend seems unlikely.

It is claimed, too, that ranchers who gave him food and shelter knew who he was. Odd, since no one had seen the bandit's face. True or not, he was cared for at the isolated ranches, and no questions were asked.

He was captured, of course, tried and sentenced to a life-term in the penitentiary at Rawlins, Wyoming. He knew he had it coming.

He never explained why he didn't take a train out of the country. He did say he had never walked into the Casper newspaper office to put an item in the paper, nor had he sent a message to the U.P. officials, nor had he been in the various places where he "had been seen," much less sitting in a Casper barber chair while the county sheriff discussed the "notorious criminal."

"I was always in the ranching area round Laramie Peak," he stated.

He *did* say he could have been the desperate hold-up man

as described, except he wasn't desperate nor did he want anyone hurt or killed.

While in prison he worked diligently at any task assigned to him. He made friends among the other prisoners. He used the prison library and read a lot. He learned to work with leather and sold many of the tooled products he created. In this way he was able to save about $1,000, which was his nest egg when he got out of prison. He learned to embroider, and this handiwork appeared on garments made in the prison. Some were of silk and sold well. That money went to the prison, of course. He was assigned to pack shirts into the crates that took them out to the dealers.

This last task presented an opportunity for escape. He took it. He concealed himself in a crate of shirts along with tools to open the crate and items he would need outside the prison.

He was soon free, leaving red-faced prison officials in his wake trying to solve the riddle of his escape.

He foolishly dared another hold-up and when a passenger pulled a gun he tried to wrestle it away. The gun went off. The bullet went into his right hand. No one else was hurt.

Carlisle got away, his bleeding hand left a bright trail easy to follow. He was back in custody within two days. He'd received another gun-shot wound when a jittery sheriff fired at him when the terrible outlaw didn't raise his injured hand high enough when ordered.

"I thought he was going for a gun," the sheriff said.

Carlisle's injured right hand was wrapped in blood-soaked bandages; he was plainly suffering and unable to use the arm. It seems unlikely that he made a threatening movement with the arm. But the sheriff shot him. The bullet struck him in the right lung.

It was 1919. There were few cars in the country at that time. Carlisle was bundled onto a horse and the posse plodded across the rough winter-seized country to the hospital in Douglas, Wyoming.

The criminal developed pneumonia and for some time it was a question whether he could survive. Meanwhile he was warm and fed and had the caring he had sought all his life. When he was sufficiently recovered, he was returned to prison at Rawlins.

As the heavy door slammed shut behind the handsome Bill Carlisle, he may have felt a little sorry for himself. He would spend the rest of his life behind bars for relieving a few train passengers of less than one thousand dollars. These same passengers, along with some not even involved, filed reimbursement claims with the railroad company for many times the amount of money that had been put into the porter's cap. In addition, Carlisle's name was blackened, and he would carry the brand of "criminal" for the balance of his life.

But Carlisle did not dwell on that. He set to work again in the prison, obeying orders, studying, working at leathercraft, and selling what he could. With money obtained from those sales, he bought a typewriter and took a correspondence course in bookkeeping.

"I must give credit for the turn-around to Father Gerard Schellinger," he said years later. "He was very kind and helpful. He worked hard to get my sentence reduced, and later worked for a full pardon for me. He even offered to serve time in my place if ever I went wrong again. With someone like that willing to trust you—well, what can you do? You certainly can't let them down!"

In 1936 Bill Carlisle walked out of prison, a free man and a Catholic convert, determined to become a responsible citizen.

He bought and operated a candy and cigar store in Kemmerer, Wyoming. He was doing quite well when a misbehaving appendix sent him to the hospital. There he met and fell in love with Lillian Berquist, an attractive red-haired nurse. After his recovery, the couple was married. Later the same year they moved to Laramie, and some years later they adopted a little girl.

The one-time outlaw first leased, and then purchased the first tourist camp set up in Laramie. The name was changed from Spring Creek Auto Camp to "Bill's Cottage Camp" and later to "The Lone Bandit."

Operating a tourist camp was much different from embroidering pansies on silk pajamas or selling cigars and leathercraft. The Carlisles operated the tourist portion and leased out the second floor dining room. The dining room soon became the preferred eating place in Laramie.

In 1947, Governor Lester Hunt acceded to Father Schellinger's requests and granted a full and unconditional pardon to the one-time "desperate outlaw."

The pardon was a surprise to the Carlisles, although they knew the priest was working for it. They accepted this gift with unconcealed emotion and gratitude to their friend, the priest.

In 1956, the couple sold their tourist camp. The new owners renamed it "The Round-Up." The place remained an interesting landmark on the east edge of Laramie until 1975 when two doctors purchased it. It has since become a small-shopping center known as Aspen Plaza. Only the legend of the Lone Bandit, Bill Carlisle, now remains.

∽

BIBLIOGRAPHICAL ESSAY. Carlisle's autobiography, *The Lone Bandit,* (Pasadena, California: Trail End Publishing Company, 1946) provided many details.

Newspaper items and day-to-day reports of the search for and tactics of Bill Carlisle as printed in the daily editions of the *Laramie Republican,* the *Casper Tribune,* the *Sheridan Enterprise,* all Wyoming papers, and the *Rocky*

Mountain News and *Denver Post,* both published in Denver, also gave accounts of Carlisle's crimes.

My article on historic homes, "The Round-Up, Laramie's First Tourist Camp," published June 5, 1977, in the *Laramie Boomerang Picket Pin* spurred my interest in Carlisle.

ᏭᎧ ᏭᎧ ᏭᎧ ᏭᎧ ᏭᎧ ᏭᎧ ᏭᎧ ᏭᎧ ᏭᎧ ᏭᎧ ᏭᎧ ᏭᎧ ᏭᎧ ᏭᎧ ᏭᎧ

FROM THE *MEDICINE BOW* (WYOMING) *POST*

RESIDENT CALLED TO REPORT A LIGHT IN THE MUSEUM [THE OLD RAILROAD DEPOT] AND A STRANGE SHAPE OF A "MAN WITH NO HEAD" IN THE WINDOW. INVESTIGATION SHOWED THE "GHOST" WAS A MANNIKIN.

SPECULATION WAS THAT IT COULD BE THE "GENTLEMAN BANDIT," RETURNED TO HIS OLD STOMPING GROUND, LOOKING FOR A TRAIN TO ROB. THE "GENTLEMAN BANDIT" WAS ANOTHER NAME GIVEN TO BILL CARLISLE WHO ROBBED ONLY MEN PASSENGERS ON THE TRAINS.

ᏭᎧ ᏭᎧ ᏭᎧ ᏭᎧ ᏭᎧ ᏭᎧ ᏭᎧ ᏭᎧ ᏭᎧ ᏭᎧ ᏭᎧ ᏭᎧ ᏭᎧ ᏭᎧ ᏭᎧ

✠ Murder!

THE WOMAN WAS small and couldn't have given much resistance to an assailant. She was Mrs. Ludwig (Louis) Wurl. She had been attacked when she entered the barn at the family ranch, her head brutally struck with a rock. Then her assassin struck her repeatedly in the face with a shovel, smashing her features almost beyond recognition. Not satisfied with this mutilation, or possibly fearing that she would not die before she was found, the fiend cut her throat. Oddly, all three weapons were left in plain sight at the scene. The shovel was neatly returned to its usual place.

Her husband, Louis, found her lying on the barn floor when he put up his team of horses.

"I had called out, at the house, that I was home," he told the sheriff. "There was no answer, so I went on to the barn to tend to the team. I called again for Minnie, then saw her lying there on the floor—beaten—and bloody—and found she was dead."

According to newspaper reports at the time [October 1896], Wurl then hurried the half-mile to his sister's ranch home and had his nephew go to Tie Siding to telegraph the sheriff at Laramie City.

Sheriff M.N. Grant and Coroner Miller drove as quickly as possible from Laramie to the Wurl Ranch, and there found the distraught Wurl.

∞ Minnie Wurl was attacked and killed in the barn at the family ranch. (Beery Collection)

The handsome German told the sheriff that he had left home the previous morning about 10:30 to haul a load of hay to Laramie. He had put up at the Kuster Hotel and started home about 1:30 the following afternoon.

"As I drove through the meadow," he told the sheriff, "I saw cattle there where they shouldn't be. When I reached the yard and went to the house and called out, there was no reply, I went to unhitch and put the team away, and as I entered the barn and called out for Minnie, I saw two milk cows in the barn—they shouldn't be there that time of day. Then I saw Minnie lying on the barn floor...."

The Laramie newspaper, the *Boomerang*, stated that the Wurl Ranch was located about two miles northeast of Tie Siding on a rocky hillside near the head of Harney Creek. The buildings were about two miles from the railroad, out of sight in a cove, and could not be seen from the neighboring ranches.

Other ranchers in the area were Wurl's brother William, their brother-in-law Fred Borgeman, and W.J. Broadhurst. Wurl told Sheriff Grant that Minnie was headed to the Broadhurst Ranch when he left for Laramie City. Mrs. Broadhurst said that Minnie stayed at her place until about 2:30 that Monday afternoon, then left for home. She was walking.

It appeared that Minnie started a fire in the kitchen stove against the October chill and probably to begin preparing supper. Then she changed into her working clothes. The garments she had worn to the neighbors' lay on the bed. She then went to the barn to begin evening chores and there met her death.

Examination of the barn, the yard and house gave few clues. The murder weapons, almost as if deliberately planted, were all in plain sight. There were few footprints in the yard. The general disarray of the household furnishings, and the tumbled bedclothes gave evidence that a search had been made. It was generally known that the Wurls kept money in the house. Wurl said that ninety dollars they had hidden was gone.

This immediately gave rise to suspicion that the motive was robbery. But then, why had the murder occurred in the barn? No other clues were found. The beaten and bloody body, the bloody weapons with gore and hair clinging to them, no other evidence—the lady had not been violated.

The inquest turned up no clue. The brutal deed held the community in its grip of horror for weeks while Grant sifted and searched for further clues.

The *Boomerang* blared "Someone should come to the Sheriff's rescue and *do* something to stop crime in this section. The officer that Albany County needs worse than any other is a sheriff."

Days followed with no clue. Even the talented armchair sleuths gave no help, but speculation and gossip soon took over. Tales were abundant.

Could this foul deed have been done by Minnie's ex-husband, a man named Olvis? The newspaper account related that "...it was known Minnie and Olvis had lived on a ranch out on Sand Creek, that their marriage was stormy and noisy and unhappy. That in a great rage after one battle, Olvis had walked away, swearing vengeance against Minnie." It was also stated that Olvis had left the country in 1883 and returned to Wisconsin. [A search of public records reveals no person named Olvis lived in the Sand Creek area during that time.] It was also stated that Minnie obtained a divorce and that she and Wurl were then married.

Minnie and Louis were married August 19, 1881, in Laramie with William Wurl and Fred Pilger as witnesses.

Even if the man Olvis had sworn vengeance, it seems improbable that anyone could nurse anger and hatred for thirteen long years. Public speculation turned elsewhere.

Two rewards were posted for five hundred dollars each. One by the Sheriff and County Commissioners, the other by Louis Wurl and his brother William. There were no claimants.

One of the stories that gossip rolled over the tongue was that Minnie's father and Wurl's father (or Olvis's in some versions) had decreed that their children should wed. Minnie had objected furiously; the gossip didn't deal with the feelings of Wurl or Olvis on the matter. The tale went on to relate that the couple had been locked in a bedroom overnight, thus making a shotgun wedding necessary. "She made life miserable for him." "They fought constantly." It made interesting talk, whether true or not.

One might question the story. Minnie, according to family records, was born in 1842. There is no record of when she married Olvis. But by the time she married Wurl, Minnie would hardly have been of an age to be forced into an unwilling alliance. She was thirty-nine.

So little by little talk died down. But suspicion didn't.

It gradually swung toward Louis Wurl himself. It was pretty well known that he had a more-than-passing attraction to another man's wife—Mrs. Otto Krueger—and the newspaper remarked, "Wurl would probably be pleased if circumstances eliminated Minnie."

Wurl was again questioned closely. He stuck by his story, pointing out that his team had been in town all night, he was registered at the Kuster Hotel, he had been seen about town at the places he normally frequented....

Yes, doubters said, that may all be true...but *maybe* he had brought an extra horse to town with him, left it out at the fairgrounds? (The fairgrounds were on east Grand Avenue at that time.) Or *maybe* he had an accomplice who loaned him a saddle horse?

Maybe he had hopped a train out and back. There were plenty of trains running, and who would see him hiking from the railroad to the ranch in the dark? Or even in late afternoon. It was only two miles. The ranch was out of sight of all neighbors, even out of sight of the railroad.

But he was registered at the Kuster, manager Peter Smart had bid him goodnight, saw him go upstairs. Sure, but what about the "ladies" entrance at the back of the hotel....

On and on the gossip flew.

His friends contended that Wurl was not guilty. Couldn't be! A fine, upstanding citizen, pillar of the community and his church, elected to the State Legislature in 1893, served until 1895. He couldn't have done such a foul deed!

So talk again died down. But it was revived again when a few months later Louis Wurl left the country. He sold his dairy ranch to brother William and struck out. With him went Mrs. Otto Krueger and three of her five children, two boys and the little girl.

∞ Louis Wurl committed suicide in 1898, overcome with remorse for having murdered his wife. (Beery Collection)

Later it was learned that they had gone to the Boer settlement in South Africa.

Some years later a letter from Marie Krueger informed relatives in Laramie that Louis had committed suicide in 1898, overcome by remorse for having murdered Minnie. She stated that her small daughter had died in Africa, that she and the two boys had been deported back to her old home in Germany when the British had moved to that part of Africa.

So the slaying of Minnie Wurl was apparently solved at last.

A curious aftermath to the murder was a tale frequently told by old-time railroaders.

The Union Pacific tracks passed the Wurl ranch on a curve, but out of sight of the buildings. Engineer Tom McHugh declared that whenever his locomotive approached that curve, Mrs. Wurl appeared on the running board (or cow-catcher) and rode around the curve, then disappeared.

The engineer was known as an unusually level-headed, practical man, and rational in every other way. But he declared firmly that Mrs. Wurl rode the running-board of his engine. So shaken was he by this happenstance that he asked and was granted transfer.

When he was relieved of that run, he asked his replacement "Does Mrs. Wurl ride with you?"

"No. Never," was the reply.

"Strange," McHugh mused. "She always rode with me."

❋

There exists another version to that spine-tingling tale:

Louis Wurl, an especially handsome man, broke up the marriage of Minnie and the man named Olvis in Wisconsin. Olvis sued for divorce, naming Wurl as respondent.

In 1880 Wurl came to Laramie where he had relatives. Whether Minnie came with him at that time is not known, but they were married in Laramie August 19, 1881, and settled on their ranch. There they operated a dairy.

This tale states that Minnie disappeared and her body was discovered sometime later beneath the barn floor. Her ghost appeared on the train from the time of her disappearance until her body was discovered, then it disappeared.

This is not the story reported in the newspapers, however. Whichever version is believed, it still presents a gruesome picture of life in Wyoming in the late nineteenth century.

∞

BIBLIOGRAPHICAL ESSAY. Special permission was given by Dicksie Knight May, official historian of the Wurl families, to relate the story. She had heard the story of the "forced wedding" between Minnie and Wurl, but stated it was not true. The marriage certificate for the pair (Albany County records) shows Minnie was "over 21." Family records indicate she was born in 1842, so she would have been 39 when she married Wurl.

Information was obtained from other family members: Harriet McCormick, Steve Grobrowski, and LeRoy Krueger, a former resident of Laramie now living in Oregon.

Newspapers furnished other information, particularly Laramie's *Boomerang* of pertinent dates in 1896.

The story of Mrs. Wurl's ghost was found in John C. Thompson's column "In Old Wyoming" in a Cheyenne paper, and also related by LeRoy Krueger.

✿ STILL WATERS

"**P**ROHIBITION NEVER bothered Laramie," the Old Timer recalled with a grin. "We stayed wet. Booze was easy to come by, and the law wasn't really strict most of the time. Seemed like everybody had a still. There were plenty out in the mountains, and Boulder Ridge was just crawling with them. Well, plenty in the valley, too. I remember one place that was hidden in the bank of the Pioneer Canal. I don't think the fellow was ever caught. Whenever there was to be a raid *some* body got the word out, and the still was covered up or the liquor moved. This fellow just turned his brew in to the irrigation ditch and fed the mash to his livestock. Never had any problems.

"One rancher named Gundlach lived out north of town. He was visited and thirty gallons of mash liberated. I remember that being in the newspaper. That was back in March 1923.

"All through the twenties and thirties and even into the 1940s the bootlegging went on. Prohibition went into effect in 1919, I believe, and it was repealed in 1933. Lasted thirteen years and a few months, but in that time there was plenty of money made here. While there were no fortunes made, it did bring in much needed dough. Remember the Depression was real deep during the thirties. That was the dry Dust Bowl years, and we couldn't raise much—it was a rough period

261

even after we got into the war in '42. The Depression drug on
for a long time into the forties, so the war didn't solve many
problems.

"Of course there was the 3.2, but most folks preferred
their home brew. They thought 3.2 was a little too fresh.
When the prohibition bill went into effect the saloons closed
up—up front, that is. The back rooms ran wide open. They
called them speakeasies or blind pigs, like in the east—or just
card rooms."

"Were there other places besides the old saloons where
you could get booze?"

"Oh, sure! There were private sources, lots of people had
a special supplier. One fellow I know had a standing order for
a gallon of whiskey a week. It was some of the best. Bill
Powell's, I believe. His was just about the best recipe going.

"Then there were some roadhouses. Dance halls we
called them, mostly, but liquor could be had there as well as
dancing and partying. One of the good spots was out east of
town, called the Moonlight. It was a roadhouse, dancing, partying, probably cards and liquor. Not really a bad place, but
lots of girls who went out for the dancing didn't like it
known they ever were there. Kind of a questionable reputation, I guess. Another well-known spot was the Triangle Tav-
ern. It was north, where the road turns toward Sybille
Canyon, known as the Wheatland Cutoff. The place burned
down. And right here in town, the best known of all was the
old Community Hall over in West Laramie. It still stands, but
it's closed up tight now.

"Now *that* was a lively place. Dances every Saturday
night, usually with a fight or two. Liquor flowed pretty freely
over there, and whenever there was a fight the crowd would
go outside to watch. When it was over, they'd all come back
in and go back to dancing. If a fight broke out inside the hall,

∾ Louis and Minnie Wurl (see "Murder!") *are included in a group having a sample from a moonshine still.* (Beery Collection)

dancing went on anyway. They'd turn the piano around and the band would sit behind it and keep right on playing. That was a lively place! Because of the fights the place was called the Bucket of Blood."

The Laramie *Republican* reported that a man named Conley had been hauled in for selling liquor without a license to soldiers at the maneuver-camp over in the Laramie Range.

He protested. He declared he did not have a moonshine still in a mountain stream with the smokestack sticking up through the water. He said he did not sell liquor of any kind to any of the three witnesses who testified for the government. But he was charged with selling two dollars worth of liquor to George Page and another two dollars worth to a John Doe, a soldier. "Doe" and another soldier gave "positive evidence" and Conley was fined two hundred dollars on each count.

According to the paper, Conley stated he "wasn't running a mountain moonshine distillery and hardly thought he could sell whiskey at a buck, six bits a quart made from corn hauled over the U.P. and then out into the mountains."

"Of course most of this activity was during the twenties and thirties. I remember a little old man who lived out east of town in a dugout and raised hogs. He also made liquor. He had a four-wheel cart and hitched a six-dog team to it and hauled his goods to town. After he made his deliveries, he'd go up and down the alleys and collect garbage that the cafes and restaurants threw out and take it out to feed his hogs.

"Then there was a house over on South Second that was always watched. The Feds seized 230 bottles of beer from the lady. She had to pay a fine for possessing and selling. And just the month before she'd been fined a hundred dollars for the same thing. The newspapers were full of such reports. There were two fellows on North Pine who were fined for possession and selling. The paper said 1227 bottles of liquor were found. I always thought that was an exaggeration— more like 227. But anyway, all but a few bottles were broken. The rest was taken for evidence."

"Did the evidence survive?" I asked.

"We-ell—," the Old Timer chuckled.

"You mentioned Boulder Ridge—" I hinted.

"Lots of stills out there! Seemed like every family had one. Some comical things went on out there, too. I remember a bunch of cattle got into the rancher's still. They really went to work on it, and you never saw a drunker herd of cattle in your life! Staggerin' all over the pasture—not a pain in the bunch, but boy, were they confused!

"Then there was the rancher who liked to entertain his company. He'd catch an old rooster and feed him home brew from a teaspoon then turn him loose. It was a real circus watching that bird stagger around. And he always went after the hens!"

"Wasn't George Trabing a federal agent sometime back in the twenties?"

"No. He was sheriff. His son Vern was the agent later on. Well, yeah, George Trabing was county sheriff and his brother-in-law, Jess Oakley, was his deputy. Jess told about stills being hid all over the country. He said that during the two years he served with Trabing they destroyed ninety-four stills. They smashed the machinery and dumped the liquor. One big outfit they hauled to town for evidence. There was a picture of it in the Laramie *Boomerang* back in the late twenties. The paper told that the sheriff had brought a keg of whiskey back as evidence and stored it in the women's ward at the jail. One hundred and sixty proof alcohol, the paper said. It was green and blew out the plug in the keg. Prisoners in the men's section managed to dangle a cup over the partition and catch a lot of the evidence. There was a bunch of drunk prisoners there for awhile! Plenty of the stuff blew up because it was green. One house was knocked off its foundation when a batch blew up. It just didn't get enough age on it before it gave up the ghost.

"Like I said, the saloons closed up front, but the back rooms run wide open. Many of the bootleggers put their stuff in wide mouth fruit jars. They'd leave the jars in roadside culverts or along beside fence posts and their customers could pick it up. This way the supplier could deliver without being seen. It was said that of all the liquor available Billy Powell's was the preferred brew. Guess they thought his recipe was best."

"Powell got into a lot of trouble with the agents, didn't he?"

"Yes, he did. They prowled over his land every few days. They found and destroyed a lot of liquor, but never seemed satisfied that they'd found it all. One of the men I knew who had helped the agents asked Powell about it later. Powell laughed and told him they walked right over it whenever they came onto the place. 'How so?' my friend asked. And Powell told him it was hidden beneath the path.

"Another advantage to using the fruit jars, the boys in the back rooms would line the jars up along the floor and when the agents came to tip over the joint, all that was necessary was to kick over the glass jars and the liquid assets would drain away through cracks in the floor. If there was time, they'd hose down the floor, or spill some vinegar around.

"My grandparents had a hay ranch out west of Laramie. They had a couple of hands who drove a Model T Ford roadster without a top. I think I was in seventh heaven when they let me go to town with them one time…. It was dark when we came home, and they stopped off to pick up a case of home brew. The roads were dirt and pitted and rutted, and I think we hit every bump there was between town and the ranch. The car lights weren't much good, so we got shook up pretty good, and pretty soon we heard a bunch of explosions. We were sure someone was shooting at us, and the faster we drove the more explosions we heard behind us. That was one of the wildest rides I have ever had. I was ten or twelve and scared just about out of my shoes. When we got home and the fellas looked at their booze, they found it was the bottles blowing up we had heard. They'd got a case of green stuff.

"One of the tales I always got a kick out of had to do with G.R. McConnell—ever heard of him?"

"Wasn't he an attorney?"

"Yes—*quite* an attorney! Well, he was representing a well known bootlegger and there was a flask half full of whiskey entered as evidence. G.R. picked it up and showed it to the court, jury and company. He said, 'Now we have here in evidence this half-pint of what is said to be whiskey. My client says it isn't. If it's not whiskey, could it then be poison? So we have a point to settle. Is this whiskey or is it poison? Would members of the jury taste it and tell us what it is?'

"None of the jury would. So G.R. turned to the judge and asked if he would care to taste and tell what it was. No, the judge wouldn't.

"'But we must know what we have here as evidence. No member of the jury wishes to taste it, nor does His Honor. Therefore, I shall have to.' G.R. drank that half-pint of liquor and smacked his lips. 'It's whiskey all right, but Your Honor, I see here no evidence of moonshining, so I move the case against my client be dismissed.'

"The Judge could do nothing else but dismiss, and G.R. hurried out of the courtroom and passed out in the hall, dead drunk!"

"Mr. McConnell was some lawyer!"

The Old Timer grinned and lifted an empty hand in mock toast.

"I'll drink to that!"

⟋

BIBLIOGRAPHICAL ESSAY. Although this tale may read like fiction, every bit is true and tells only in small part of goings-on during that interesting period of our history.

Many of these facts were gleaned from Laramie's two newspapers before they were merged: the *Republican* and the *Boomerang*.

The Old Timer is a composite of the following persons: Louis Lutz, Fred Dudley, Albert Melcher, Blake Fanning, Dorothy Mason, Dorothy Cameron, Dicksie K. May, all of Laramie, and LeRoy Krueger, former Laramie resident, now living in Oregon. Others who contributed wish to remain nameless. My gratitude and appreciation go to all.

INDEX

⚭

Author Gladys Beery

Gladys B. Beery was born in northeastern Nebraska. At the age of two weeks, she moved with her parents to Montana. Later the family moved to northeastern Colorado, then to central Nebraska where she met her future husband, Lloyd Beery. In 1956 the Beerys moved, with their three children, to Laramie, Wyoming.

During the years when she worked in the offices of the Albany County Engineer and County Clerk and Recorder, she became interested in the history of Wyoming and the city of Laramie. This interest brought about a series of stories on the historic homes of Laramie which was published in the *Laramie Daily Boomerang* and its supplement *The Picket Pin.*

Research on the houses led to compiling a history of the city as told in *The Front Streets of Laramie City* and later to the historical fiction *Mule Woman.*

Beery's works have appeared in the *Laramie Daily Boomerang, True West, Far West, Owen Wister Review, Ghost Town Quarterly* and various anthologies, including poets' collections.

She is currently working on a book of western fiction.

*This book is printed on
60-pound Thor White
recycled, acid free paper.*